JOHN

SIGNS OF THE MESSIAH

JOHN

SIGNS OF THE MESSIAH

STORYTELLER

Lifeway Press®
Brentwood, Tennessee

Editorial Team

Ben Reed
Devotional writer

Stephanie Cross
Associate Editor

Angel Prohaska
Assistant Editor

Reid Patton
Senior Editor

Jon Rodda
Art Director

Tyler Quillet
Managing Editor

Joel Polk
Publisher, Small Group Publishing

John Paul Basham
Director, Adult Ministry Publishing

ISBN: 978-1-0877-8357-4 • Item number: 005842044
Dewey decimal classification: 226.5 • Subject heading: BIBLE / GOSPELS AND ACTS / JOHN

All Scripture quotations are taken from the Christian Standard Bible®, Copyright © 2017 by Holman Bible Publishers. Used by permission. Christian Standard Bible® and CSB® are federally registered trademarks of Holman Bible Publishers.

To order additional copies of this resource, write to Lifeway Resources Customer Service; 200 Powell Place, Suite 100, Brentwood, TN 27027; fax 615-251-5933; call toll free 800-458-2772; order online at Lifeway.com; or email orderentry@lifeway.com.

Printed in the United States of America

Adult Ministry Publishing • Lifeway Resources • 200 Powell Place • Brentwood, TN 37027

CONTENTS

WEEK 1

WEEK 2

WEEK 3

WEEK 4

WEEK 5

WEEK 6

WEEK 7

ABOUT STORYTELLER

God could've chosen to reveal Himself in any way that He desired, yet in His wisdom, He chose to reveal Himself in the context of a story. We come to know and understand this reality as we immerse ourselves in the Scriptures and begin to see the entirety of Scripture as one interconnected story. By becoming familiar with the individual stories of Scripture, we train ourselves to see each as one part of God's big story.

Storyteller: John is a seven-week devotional and group Bible study experience designed to take people through Scripture in a way that is beautiful, intuitive, and interactive. Each volume uses a book of the Bible or a portion of Scripture from within a book to examine a key theme. This theme guides the Bible study experience and gives readers handles to help understand and digest what they're reading.

At the end of each study, your should have a deeper understanding of God, His Word, the big themes of Scripture, the connectedness of God's story, and His work in your life.

Let's enter the story together.

ABOUT JOHN

The Gospel of John is different from the Synoptic Gospels—Matthew, Mark, and Luke—in that more than 90 percent of its material is unique. John's Gospel does not focus on the miracles, parables, and public speeches that are so prominent in the other accounts. Instead, the Gospel of John emphasizes the identity of Jesus as the Son of God and how we, as believers, should respond to His teachings.

AUTHOR

A close reading of the Gospel of John suggests that the author was an apostle (1:14); one of the Twelve ("the disciple Jesus loved," 13:23; 19:26; 20:2; 21:20); and, still more specifically, John, the son of Zebedee. The early church also held that the apostle John was the author of this Gospel.

DATE AND CIRCUMSTANCES OF WRITING

John was likely written in the period between AD 70 (the date of the destruction of the temple) and 100 (the end of John's lifetime), with a date in the 80s most likely. The testimony of the early church also favors a date after AD 70.

The most likely place of writing is Ephesus, one of the most important urban centers of the Roman Empire at the time, though the envisioned readership of John's Gospel transcends any one historical setting.

John's original audience was probably composed of people in the larger Greco-Roman world in Ephesus and beyond toward the close of the first century AD. This is likely why John frequently explained Jewish customs and Palestinian geography and translated Aramaic terms into Greek.

MESSAGE AND EMPHASIS

The purpose statement in 20:30-31 indicates that John wrote with an evangelistic purpose, probably seeking to reach unbelievers through Christian readers of his Gospel. If the date of composition was after AD 70, the time of the destruction of the Jerusalem temple, it is likely that John sought to present Jesus as the new temple and center of worship for God's people in replacement of the old sanctuary.

John emphasized the deity of Jesus from the beginning of his Gospel. Jesus used the significant phrase "I am" seven times in John, claiming the personal name of God as His own. In John, Jesus is always in charge and knows what will happen in advance.

Knowing and believing are key terms for John. Both occur more than ninety times in this Gospel and are always used as verbs. Jesus's teaching in John reminds us that knowing God and believing in Jesus are expressed in action.

CONTRIBUTION TO THE BIBLE

Of all the Gospels and any of the New Testament books, the Gospel of John most clearly teaches the deity and preexistence of Christ (1:1-2,18; 8:58; 17:5,24; 20:28). Together with the Gospel of Matthew, it provides the most striking proofs of Jesus's messiahship. Jesus's messianic mission is shown to originate with God the Father, "the One who sent" Jesus (7:16,18,28,33; 8:26,29; 15:21), and to culminate in His commissioning of His new messianic community in the power of His Spirit (20:21-22).[2]

WHY STUDY JOHN?

The Gospel of John is one of four books that describes the life of Jesus. Matthew, Mark, and Luke are known as Synoptic Gospels because they use many of the same events and lay them out much the same way. John's Gospel follows a different outline and includes much material that is not covered in the other three Gospels. John's thesis statement is recorded near the end of the book:

> [30] Jesus performed many other signs in the presence of his disciples that are not written in this book. [31] But these are written so that you may believe that Jesus is the Messiah, the Son of God, and that by believing you may have life in his name.
> —JOHN 20:30-31

John's Gospel is organized in two big sections: the book of the signs and the book of the exaltation. Both ask us to examine the evidence about Jesus, believe, and find life in His name. The book of the signs is the focus of this study, and it introduces us to Jesus through the lens of seven key miracles or signs that He performed to disclose His identity and prove His divinity. These signs are meant to show us who Jesus is and what He is like. They disclose to us what He cares about and point us back to God. For all of us following Jesus, and those who are just looking into who Jesus is, these signs lead us on a path to the Savior.

Meet Jesus. See Jesus. Believe in Jesus. Find life in His name.

OUTLINE OF JOHN

I. The Prologue (1:1-18)

II. The Book of the Signs (1:19–12:50)

    A. The Forerunner and the Coming of the Messiah (1:19-51)

        1. The Testimony of John the Baptist (1:19-34)

        2. The Beginning of Jesus's Ministry (1:35-51)

    B. The Cana Cycle: Jesus's Inaugural Signs and Conversations (2–4)

        1. Sign 1: Changing Water into Wine at the Wedding in Cana (2:1-12)

        2. The Clearing of the Temple (2:13-22)

        3. Conversations: Nicodemus, and the Samaritan Woman (2:23–4:42)

        4. Sign 2: The Healing of the Royal Official's Son (4:43-54)

    C. The Festival Cycle: Additional Signs amid Mounting Unbelief (5–10)

        1. Sign 3: Healing of the Lame Man (5:1-47)

        2. Sign 4: Feeding the Five Thousand (6:1-15)

        3. Sign 5: Walking on Water (6:16-21)

        3. Bread of Life Discourse (6:22-71)

        4. Jesus at the Festival of Shelters (7–8)

        5. Sign 6: The Healing of the Blind Man (9)

        7. Good Shepherd Discourse (10)

    D. Final Passover and Other Events (11–12)

        1. Sign 7: The Raising of Lazarus (11)

        2. Final Events of Jesus's Public Ministry (12)[1]

HOW TO USE THIS STUDY

Each week follows a repeated rhythm to guide you in your study
of John and was crafted with lots of white space and photographic
imagery to facilitate a time of reflection on Scripture.

The week begins with an
introduction to the themes
of the week. Throughout
each week you'll find
Scripture readings, devotions,
and beautiful imagery to
guide your time.

WEEK 1

FOLLOW ME

Each week includes five days
of Scripture reading along with
a short devotional thought
and three questions to process
what you've read.

The Scripture reading is printed
out for you with plenty of
space for you to take notes,
circle, underline, and interact
with the passage.

The sixth day contains no reading beyond a couple of verses to give you time to pause and listen to what God has said through the Scriptures this week. You may be tempted to skip this day all together, but resist this temptation. Sit and be quiet with God—even if it's only for a few minutes.

The seventh day each week offers a list of open-ended questions that apply to any passage of Scripture. Use this day to reflect on your own or meet with a group to discuss what you've learned. Take intentional time to remember and reflect on what the story of John is teaching you.

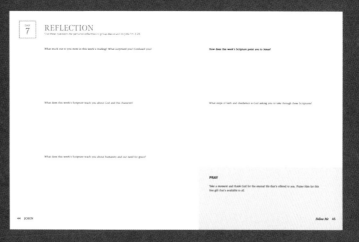

Throughout each week of study, you will notice callout boxes or supplemental pages provided to give greater context and clarity to the Scripture you're reading. These features will help you connect John to the bigger story of Scripture.

LEADING A GROUP

Each week of study contains a set of questions that can be used for small group meetings. These open-ended questions are meant to guide discussion of the week's Scripture passage. No matter the size of your group, here are some helpful tips for guiding discussion.

PREPARE

REVIEW the Scripture and your answers to the week's questions ahead of time.

PRAY over your group as well as the Scriptures you've been studying. Ask God's Spirit for help to lead the group deeper into God's truth and deeper in relationship with one another.

MINIMIZE DISTRACTIONS

We live in a time when our attention is increasingly divided. Try to see your group time as a space and respite from the digital clutter—from scrolling, notifications, likes, and newsfeeds. Commit to one another to give focused time and attention to the discussion at hand and minimize outside distractions. Help people focus on what's most important: connecting with God, with the Bible, and with one another.

ENCOURAGE DISCUSSION

A good small group experience has the following characteristics.

EVERYONE IS INCLUDED. Your goal is to foster a community where people are welcome just as they are but encouraged to grow spiritually.

EVERYONE PARTICIPATES. Encourage everyone to ask questions, share, or read aloud.

NO ONE DOMINATES. Even though you may be "leading" the group, try to see yourself as a participant steering the conversation rather than a teacher imparting information.

DON'T RUSH. Don't feel that a moment of silence is a bad thing. People may need time, and we should be glad to give it to them. Don't feel like you have to ask all the questions or stay away from questions that aren't included. Be sensitive to the Holy Spirit and to one another. Take your time.

INPUT IS AFFIRMED AND FOLLOWED UP. Make sure you point out something true or helpful in a response. Don't just move on. Build community with follow-up questions, asking other people to share when they have experienced similar things or how a truth has shaped their understanding of God and the Scripture you're studying. Conversation stalls when people feel that you don't want to hear their answers or that you're looking for only a certain answer. Engagement and affirmation keeps the conversation going.

GOD AND HIS WORD ARE CENTRAL. The questions in this study are meant to steer the conversation back to God, His Word, and the work of the gospel in our lives. Opinions and experiences are valuable and can be helpful, but God is the center of the Bible, the center of our story, and should be the center of our discussion. Trust Him to lead the discussion. Continually point people to the Word and to active steps of faith.

KEEP CONNECTING

Spiritual growth occurs in the context of community. Think of ways to connect with group members during the week. Your group will be more enjoyable the more you get to know one another through time spent outside of an official group meeting. The more people are comfortable with and involved in one another's lives, the more they'll look forward to being together. When people move beyond being friendly to truly being friends who form a community, they come to each session eager to engage instead of merely attending. Reserve time each week to touch base with individual group members.

WEEK 1

FOLLOW ME

In the beginning was the Word.

John's Gospel begins all the way at the beginning.

Before time, before creation, before anything existed but God, we receive testimony from God that Jesus is the Son of God. He always has been. He always will be.

The testimony is followed up by the testimony of John the Baptist, who saw Jesus and declared Him to be "the Lamb of God, who takes away the sin of the world!" (1:29).

This testimony provided support as Jesus asked young men to follow Him and be His disciples. These men sensed something in Jesus that they couldn't find anywhere else. These disciples decided to "come and see" (1:46) what Jesus was doing and where He would lead.

The week culminated with the first of seven signs that demonstrate Jesus's identity. He turned water into wine at a wedding feast in a town called Cana, and then He reclaimed God's temple for God's glory.

Through this testimony and teaching, many reached John's intended conclusion and "believed in his name when they saw the signs he was doing" (2:23).

The question is, *Will you? Will you read about these signs, hear the testimony, and believe?* Come and see the heart of Jesus.

JOHN 1:1-18

1 In the beginning was the Word, and the Word was with God, and the Word was God. [2] He was with God in the beginning. [3] All things were created through him, and apart from him not one thing was created that has been created. [4] In him was life, and that life was the light of men. [5] That light shines in the darkness, and yet the darkness did not overcome it.

[6] There was a man sent from God whose name was John. [7] He came as a witness to testify about the light, so that all might believe through him. [8] He was not the light, but he came to testify about the light. [9] The true light that gives light to everyone was coming into the world.

[10] He was in the world, and the world was created through him, and yet the world did not recognize him. [11] He came to his own, and his own people did not receive him. [12] But to all who did receive him, he gave them the right to be children of God, to those who believe in his name, [13] who were born, not of natural descent, or of the will of the flesh, or of the will of man, but of God.

[14] The Word became flesh and dwelt among us. We observed his glory, the glory as the one and only Son from the Father, full of grace and truth. [15] (John testified concerning him and exclaimed, "This was the one of whom I said, 'The one coming after me ranks ahead of me, because he existed before me.'") [16] Indeed, we have all received grace upon grace from his fullness, [17] for the law was given through Moses; grace and truth came through Jesus Christ. [18] No one has ever seen God. The one and only Son, who is himself God and is at the Father's side —he has revealed him.

BACK TO THE BEGINNING

Like all stories, John starts at the beginning. Prior to John, the phrase "In the beginning" was only used one other time in Scripture—in the first line of the first book of the Bible, Genesis. At the start John takes us all the way back to the very beginning of the Bible, to the very beginning of time itself.

But John uses these words in his prologue for different reasons than Moses used them in Genesis. John gives us a different angle on the same story because John is telling us a specific story. He wants us to know Jesus was part of the plan from the beginning. Like God the Father, God the Son was present at the creation of the world. And in the beginning of John, we learn about a new beginning through a new covenant that will lead to new life.

Just as the original creation account in Genesis 1 took seven days, John structured the first twelve chapters of his Gospel around seven miracles, or signs, to show us Jesus's true identity as the One who is truly man and truly God. Each sign is like holding a diamond up to the light: with each turn, rather than seeing a different diamond, you see more of its beauty in this new "creation" account. Each of these signs is concluded with a report letting us know how the people responded to Jesus.

In stark contrast to gods worshiped by the broader culture at the time of the writing, we see that the Word (Jesus) descended from His throne to live among us (see John 1:14). Jesus is a wholly different ruler, the face and embodiment of God the Father. He wasn't simply staying in heaven, doling out rules and tasks. Culturally and theologically different than what most expected, Jesus is "the true light that gives light to everyone" (1:9). That light didn't just extend to first-century readers: you and I aren't beyond this Light's reach. He is being revealed to us in the pages of John's Gospel.

Jesus was the plan from the beginning.

REFLECTIONS

Take some time to read Genesis 1:1-31. What connections can you make between Genesis 1 and John 1?

According to John 1:12-13, what does it mean to be a child of God? How does someone step into that relationship?

CONNECTING THE STORY

This section, known as John's prologue, intentionally pulls themes and language from the first chapter of the Bible, Genesis 1. There we learn that God created the universe and everything in it from nothing through an act of His will. Here we learn that Jesus is God and was with God in the beginning. From the outset of John's Gospel, there is no denying Jesus's identity.

JOHN 1:19-42

JOHN THE BAPTIST'S TESTIMONY

19 This was John's testimony when the Jews from Jerusalem sent priests and Levites to ask him, "Who are you?"

20 He didn't deny it but confessed, "I am not the Messiah."

21 "What then?" they asked him. "Are you Elijah?"

"I am not," he said.

"Are you the Prophet?"

"No," he answered.

22 "Who are you, then?" they asked. "We need to give an answer to those who sent us. What can you tell us about yourself?"

23 He said, "I am a **voice of one crying out in the wilderness: Make straight the way of the Lord** — just as Isaiah the prophet said."

24 Now they had been sent from the Pharisees. 25 So they asked him, "Why then do you baptize if you aren't the Messiah, or Elijah, or the Prophet?"

26 "I baptize with water," John answered them. "Someone stands among you, but you don't know him. 27 He is the one coming after me, whose sandal strap I'm not worthy to untie." 28 All this happened in Bethany across the Jordan, where John was baptizing.

THE LAMB OF GOD

29 The next day John saw Jesus coming toward him and said, "Look, the Lamb of God, who takes away the sin of the world! 30 This is the one I told you about: 'After me comes a man who ranks ahead of me, because he existed before me.' 31 I didn't know him, but I came baptizing with water so that he might be revealed to Israel." 32 And John testified, "I saw the Spirit descending from heaven like a dove, and he rested on him. 33 I didn't know him, but he who sent me to baptize with water told me, 'The one you see the Spirit descending and resting on — he is the one who baptizes with the Holy Spirit.' 34 I have seen and testified that this is the Son of God."

35 The next day, John was standing with two of his disciples. 36 When he saw Jesus passing by, he said, "Look, the Lamb of God!"

37 The two disciples heard him say this and followed Jesus. 38 When Jesus turned and noticed them following him, he asked them, "What are you looking for?"

They said to him, "Rabbi" (which means "Teacher"), "where are you staying?"

39 "Come and you'll see," he replied. So they went and saw where he was staying, and they stayed with him that day. It was about four in the afternoon.

40 Andrew, Simon Peter's brother, was one of the two who heard John and followed him. 41 He first found his own brother Simon and told him, "We have found the Messiah" (which is translated "the Christ"), 42 and he brought Simon to Jesus.

When Jesus saw him, he said, "You are Simon, son of John. You will be called Cephas" (which is translated "Peter").

TESTIMONY

It had been over four hundred years since the last book of the Old Testament, Malachi, was penned. The Gospel of John picks up where Malachi left off, declaring that God would send a messenger for His people (see Malachi 3:1-2). This messenger is John the Baptist. His arrival on the scene is also a fulfillment of a prophecy in Isaiah 40:3, which John quoted in verse 23.

Biblically, a prophet is one who speaks God's words to people. And though John the Baptist stands in the line of the prophets, he is distinct. He didn't operate in the temple, but in the wilderness, bringing a message of repentance and baptism. While previous prophets had simply said, "Look to God," John the Baptist said, "God is here among us."

In this Gospel account, we learn who Jesus is through the testimony (or stories) of others. John the Baptist believed his purpose was that "[Jesus] might be revealed to Israel" (1:31). When John saw Jesus coming toward him, He declared the truth about who Jesus is, saying, "Look, the Lamb of God, who takes away the sin of the world!" (1:39).

Here we also see the story of Jesus's first disciples. They saw something so compelling and necessary in Jesus that they left everything else to follow Him. When John pointed out Jesus was the Lamb of God, Andrew was so intrigued that he went to find his brother to tell him about Jesus.

Though these accounts, we begin to see what makes Jesus different, compelling, and worth following. We begin to see what it means to have found the Messiah. And we see Jesus changing lives.

Throughout his Gospel, John gives a glimpse into the life of Jesus and invites us to come and see. When we read these stories in Scripture, that's the invitation we hear from God: "Come and you'll see." That invitation—to come and see who Jesus is and what He is doing—exists for each of us every day.

John the Baptist announced
that God was among us.

REFLECTIONS

Write out a few things you learn about Jesus from these passages. What do you learn specifically about who Jesus is?

What has Jesus done in your life? What is He showing you as you've come to Him? If this is your first time seeking Jesus, what to you hope to learn about Him?

Who might you invite to come and see Jesus with you?

JOHN 1:43-51

PHILIP AND NATHANAEL

⁴³ The next day Jesus decided to leave for Galilee. He found Philip and told him, "Follow me."

⁴⁴ Now Philip was from Bethsaida, the hometown of Andrew and Peter. ⁴⁵ Philip found Nathanael and told him, "We have found the one Moses wrote about in the law (and so did the prophets): Jesus the son of Joseph, from Nazareth."

⁴⁶ "Can anything good come out of Nazareth?" Nathanael asked him.

"Come and see," Philip answered.

⁴⁷ Then Jesus saw Nathanael coming toward him and said about him, "Here truly is an Israelite in whom there is no deceit."

⁴⁸ "How do you know me?" Nathanael asked.

"Before Philip called you, when you were under the fig tree, I saw you," Jesus answered.

⁴⁹ "Rabbi," Nathanael replied, "You are the Son of God; you are the King of Israel!"

⁵⁰ Jesus responded to him, "Do you believe because I told you I saw you under the fig tree? You will see greater things than this." ⁵¹ Then he said, "Truly I tell you, you will see heaven opened and the angels of God ascending and descending on the Son of Man."

<table>
<tr><td>DAY
3</td><td></td></tr>
</table>

THE SON OF GOD

Nicknames carry weight. How others refer to us tells us a lot about what they think of us. It also creates a reputation that we live up to—or don't live up to. They're earned over time, usually through something you did (or didn't do). Some nicknames we like and embrace, and others we reject. At times we base our identity on what people decide to call us; we choose to see ourselves how others see us.

Throughout the Bible one of the ways we learn about God is through the names and metaphors that describe His character and His nature. The Lord of Hosts, the Almighty, the Shepherd of Israel—all of these designations teach us something about God. The same is true of Jesus.

"Jesus the son of Joseph, from Nazareth" (1:45) is His given name, but that is not the whole of who Jesus is. Throughout John's Gospel and the rest of the New Testament, Jesus is given different names and designations by Himself and by others. Yesterday's reading introduced one of them—"the Lamb of God." Today's reading introduces a few more.

Jesus called Philip to follow Him, who in turn invited Nathanael along. Nathanael was skeptical and needed more proof. Yet, Jesus opened Nathanael's eyes, and we see in Nathanael's names for Jesus precisely who he believed Jesus was: "Son of God" and "King of Israel." Maybe this is how you see Jesus. Or maybe like Nathanael, you are skeptical. Jesus did something seemingly insignificant to help Nathanael see Him for who He is. To Nathanael, and to all of us, Jesus would prove over and over again that He is worthy of the titles Nathanael used. This comparatively small sign from Jesus to a new disciple was only the beginning of His miracles and signs.

As the book goes on, we will see more signs and names that give us a clearer picture of who Jesus is and what He came to accomplish.

The Lamb of God has arrived
to take away our sins.

REFLECTIONS

Based on what you know so far, who is Jesus to you?

Do you need evidence before you can trust someone? Why? How does that translate to your relationship with Jesus?

As you make your way through this study, what would it look like for you to be open to Jesus being more than you imagined?

INSIGHTS

In the first century, it was extremely common for rabbis or religious teachers to require disciples who would follow them and learn at their feet. The word *disciple* literally means "learner." As you continue though this book, notice the ways that Jesus intentionally taught and trained the disciples who followed Him.

JOHN 2:1-12

THE FIRST SIGN: TURNING WATER INTO WINE

2 On the third day a wedding took place in Cana of Galilee. Jesus's mother was there, ² and Jesus and his disciples were invited to the wedding as well. ³ When the wine ran out, Jesus's mother told him, "They don't have any wine."

⁴ "What has this concern of yours to do with me, woman?" Jesus asked. "My hour has not yet come."

⁵ "Do whatever he tells you," his mother told the servants.

⁶ Now six stone water jars had been set there for Jewish purification. Each contained twenty or thirty gallons.

⁷ "Fill the jars with water," Jesus told them. So they filled them to the brim. ⁸ Then he said to them, "Now draw some out and take it to the headwaiter." And they did.

⁹ When the headwaiter tasted the water (after it had become wine), he did not know where it came from — though the servants who had drawn the water knew. He called the groom ¹⁰ and told him, "Everyone sets out the fine wine first, then, after people are drunk, the inferior. But you have kept the fine wine until now."

¹¹ Jesus did this, the first of his signs, in Cana of Galilee. He revealed his glory, and his disciples believed in him.

¹² After this, he went down to Capernaum, together with his mother, his brothers, and his disciples, and they stayed there only a few days.

THE FIRST SIGN

We all love that part of the movie where the story begins to unfold and things start to make sense—which is exactly where we find ourselves in John 2. Jesus began to reveal His divinity, to show that He's not just another prophet, a great teacher, or a mere man.

Here we witness the first of seven signs John highlighted to prove Jesus is God. To us, turning water into wine might seem like a cool party trick or even a magic trick. Those are things that pass as "miraculous" to us. However, every time Jesus performed a miracle, He was making a claim to His identity. The miracles (or signs) in John all disclose to the people in the story (and to us) that this Man is not like other men—He does things only God can do. John tells us these signs "revealed his glory" (2:11) and led His disciples to believe in Him.

As we read, though, we realize that this isn't just some party trick or a feat to impress guests: Jesus actually turned six jars of water into six jars of wine as a demonstration of His power and divinity. The disciples' response was the intended response.

Why is turning water into wine so significant? What should have taken years to accomplish, the maturing of fine wine, Jesus accomplished in a moment. Though it may seem a small thing to us, scientists would tell you that the amount of energy needed to transform this amount of liquid would be staggering. Yet it was done without any exertion and without drawing the attention of any attendants. Jesus's ability to transform the water into wine is a glimpse into His total control over the physical world.

On the execution of this sign, Jesus revealed command and control of nature and painted the first strokes of His true identity: the Son of God.

Jesus's first miracle affirmed His identity as the Son of God.

REFLECTIONS

How would you explain the significance of this passage in your own words to someone who does not yet believe in Jesus?

How does this sign strengthen your faith?

Is there something in your life that feels like it would take years, or even decades, to untangle? Pray that the God who can turn water to wine would begin to work miraculously!

INSIGHTS

The amount of water Jesus transformed is believed to be somewhere between 120-180 gallons.

SIGNS
of the
MESSIAH

Throughout John's Gospel, Jesus performed seven signs that serve as proofs for His identity as the Son of God. They were a part of a growing body of evidence that John used to support his central goal—to have people believe in Jesus and find life in His name. Chronologically the seven signs are:

Turning Water into Wine
JOHN 2:1-12

Healing an Official's Son
JOHN 4:43-54

Healing a Disabled Man
JOHN 5:1-47

Feeding of the Five Thousand
JOHN 6:1-15

Walking on the Water
JOHN 6:16-21

Healing of the Blind Man
JOHN 9:1-12

Raising of Lazarus from the Dead
JOHN 11:1-46

JOHN 2:13-25

CLEANSING THE TEMPLE

¹³ The Jewish Passover was near, and so Jesus went up to Jerusalem. ¹⁴ In the temple he found people selling oxen, sheep, and doves, and he also found the money changers sitting there. ¹⁵ After making a whip out of cords, he drove everyone out of the temple with their sheep and oxen. He also poured out the money changers' coins and over-turned the tables. ¹⁶ He told those who were selling doves, "Get these things out of here! Stop turning my Father's house into a marketplace!"

¹⁷ And his disciples remembered that it is written: **Zeal for your house will consume me.**

¹⁸ So the Jews replied to him, "What sign will you show us for doing these things?"

¹⁹ Jesus answered, "Destroy this temple, and I will raise it up in three days."

²⁰ Therefore the Jews said, "This temple took forty-six years to build, and will you raise it up in three days?"

²¹ But he was speaking about the temple of his body. ²² So when he was raised from the dead, his disciples remembered that he had said this, and they believed the Scripture and the statement Jesus had made.

²³ While he was in Jerusalem during the Passover Festival, many believed in his name when they saw the signs he was doing. ²⁴ Jesus, however, would not entrust himself to them, since he knew them all ²⁵ and because he did not need anyone to testify about man; for he himself knew what was in man.

LIFE TO DEATH TO LIFE

Jesus went from the life of the party in John 2:1-12 to the death of another party in this passage. As He walked through the temple just before Passover, when crowds would have begun forming, He saw that the temple had become a marketplace. Instead of being a place to connect with and worship God, it was a place where goods were bought and sold.

Jesus became angry, but there's a difference between righteous and unrighteousness anger. Here, Jesus defended the dwelling place of God and the ability of all people to have access to the outer court, which should have been accessible to all who wanted to worship.

Jesus couldn't tolerate this misuse of God's temple. This truth takes on a whole new depth of meaning when Jesus calls Himself the temple in John 2:19-21. Jesus won't tolerate people using Him as an object to be traded and sold. He's the Savior of the world, not a bargaining chip.

Throughout His ministry, Jesus would continue to thwart expectations. Many Jews at the time expected the Messiah would be a military or political leader who would free them from Roman captivity. When Jesus said He's the Messiah, it's not that the people didn't believe, they were completely missing it. They were confused because this Messiah didn't line up with the one they thought would show up.

But Jesus's disciples did believe. They heard His words, saw His actions, and saw Him for who He was.

In this interchange Jesus revealed what He came to earth to accomplish: to pay for the sins of humanity by rising from the dead. His words were veiled to many, but for those who were willing to accept it, His meaning was clear. Jesus did not come to take from us as the money changers did; He came to give His life so that we might have life.

His disciples believed. They heard His words, saw His actions, and believed.

REFLECTIONS

Read John 2:25 again. How does this verse explain the way Jesus related to the crowds around Him?

The people in the temple were confused about who Jesus truly was. Is there anything you've learned about Jesus this week that challenges your previously held beliefs? Explain.

Do you know people who have some misconceptions about Jesus? How might you introduce them to the Jesus you've been learning about?

DAY
6

PAUSE & LISTEN
Spend some time reflecting over the week's reading.

In the beginning was the Word, and the Word was with God, and the Word was God. . . . In him was life, and that life was the light of men. That light shines in the darkness, and yet the darkness did not overcome it.

JOHN 1:1,4-5

REFLECTION

Use these questions for personal reflection or group discussion on John 1:1–2:25.

What stuck out to you most in this week's reading? What surprised you? Confused you?

What does this week's Scripture teach you about God and His character?

What does this week's Scripture teach you about humanity and our need for grace?

How does this week's Scripture point you to Jesus?

What steps of faith and obedience is God asking you to take through these Scriptures?

PRAY

Take a moment and thank God for the eternal life that's offered to you. Praise Him for this free gift that's available to all.

I AM HE

Listen to the One speaking.

Conversations that reset expectations were an integral part of Jesus's ministry. John's Gospel shows Jesus interacting with people from different walks of life, helping them see His true identity. This week includes two conversations with Jesus and one conversation about Jesus.

All three conversations involved resetting expectations and understanding in light of who Jesus is.

For His part, Jesus spoke with people who were not yet disciples—a Pharisee named Nicodemus and an unnamed Samaritan woman. Whether they knew it or not, both were seeking what He offered and would find their desires met in these conversations.

These were entirely different from the conversations Jesus would have with the Jewish religious leaders throughout the rest of the Gospel. These extended conversations with Jesus revealed His heart for those who are genuinely seeking and searching for Him.

They show that Jesus hears our genuine questions, receives us, and offers life in return.

JOHN 3:1-21

JESUS AND NICODEMUS

3 There was a man from the Pharisees named Nicodemus, a ruler of the Jews. ² This man came to him at night and said, "Rabbi, we know that you are a teacher who has come from God, for no one could perform these signs you do unless God were with him."

³ Jesus replied, "Truly I tell you, unless someone is born again, he cannot see the kingdom of God."

⁴ "How can anyone be born when he is old?" Nicodemus asked him. "Can he enter his mother's womb a second time and be born?"

⁵ Jesus answered, "Truly I tell you, unless someone is born of water and the Spirit, he cannot enter the kingdom of God. ⁶ Whatever is born of the flesh is flesh, and whatever is born of the Spirit is spirit. ⁷ Do not be amazed that I told you that you must be born again. ⁸ The wind blows where it pleases, and you hear its sound, but you don't know where it comes from or where it is going. So it is with everyone born of the Spirit."

⁹ "How can these things be?" asked Nicodemus.

¹⁰ "Are you a teacher of Israel and don't know these things?" Jesus replied. ¹¹ "Truly I tell you, we speak what we know and we testify to what we have seen, but you do not accept our testimony. ¹² If I have told you about earthly things and you don't believe, how will you believe if I tell you about heavenly things? ¹³ No one has ascended into heaven except the one who descended from heaven — the Son of Man.

¹⁴ "Just as Moses lifted up the snake in the wilderness, so the Son of Man must be lifted up, ¹⁵ so that everyone who believes in him may have eternal life. ¹⁶ For God loved the world in this way: He gave his one and only Son, so that everyone who believes in him will not perish but have eternal life. ¹⁷ For God did not send his Son into the world to condemn the world, but to save the world through him. ¹⁸ Anyone who believes in him is not condemned, but anyone who does not believe is already condemned, because he has not believed in the name of the one and only Son of God. ¹⁹ This is the judgment: The light has come into the world, and people loved darkness rather than the light because their deeds were evil. ²⁰ For everyone who does evil hates the light and avoids it, so that his deeds may not be exposed. ²¹ But anyone who lives by the truth comes to the light, so that his works may be shown to be accomplished by God."

A MAN OF THE PHARISEES

In the first of several interactions we'll study this week, Jesus met with a Pharisee, Nicodemus. Pharisees were a popular religious group in first-century Jerusalem known for their strict adherence to the ceremonial law. Because Nicodemus was also "a ruler of the Jews" (v. 1) he might have been representing other Pharisees as well. Their goal was to excel at keeping the law, so Nicodemus's question in verse 3 was likely a genuine one. Nicodemus coming at night also indicated He was likely seeking to have an honest conversation.

Jesus's answer to that question ripped through Pharisaical thinking, left Nicodemus perplexed, and gave us one of the best known verses in all of Scripture. The spiritual birth Jesus spoke about was a foreign concept to him.

The truth Jesus called out is that salvation is and always has been found in belief. The work we do for God does not save us—we need to be born again, which is something only God can do for us. Our sacrifices for God do not compare to the sacrifice God made on our behalf. When we believe in Jesus and look to Him for salvation, we experience new birth. This is a death to who we were and a new life found and rooted in the Messiah.

Though we're over two thousand years removed from this interaction, Nicodemus's line of thinking isn't foreign to us. We often try various means to earn God's favor, even though it is freely available to us in Jesus. Whether we're doing "good" things like reading the Bible or praying or avoiding "bad" things, we can easily fool ourselves into thinking the things we do earn us favor before God. The radical truth at the center of Christianity is that life is found in Jesus, and "everyone who believes in him will not perish but have eternal life" (v. 16).

Jesus offers the path to be born again.

REFLECTIONS

Read Numbers 21:4-9 and review John 3:14. What connections do you see between these two passages?

What are some ways you're tempted to believe that something other than faith in Jesus brings you favor with God?

INSIGHTS

The Pharisees were the ruling religious elite of the day. They believed in the oral traditions passed down through the Israelites: the Torah, the books of Wisdom, and the Prophets. They believed in the afterlife. And through their study of the Scriptures, they developed a very strict, narrow interpretation of the law. They were known to not just keep the written law but to add more laws just to keep people from potentially breaking the written law. For example, when it came to tithing (a biblical principle), they didn't just tithe on the money they received: they tithed on their individual spices and grains (see Matthew 23:23). Though well-intentioned, over time the Pharisees lost sight of why we read the Scriptures: to grow closer to God. Jesus directed much criticism toward the Pharisees.

FEATURES
of the
CANA CYCLE

The first miracle you read about on Day 4 through the reading this week (chapters 2–4 of John) is what's known as the Cana cycle, because all of the events take place in Cana of Galilee. Cana was a village in the region of Galilee. In these chapters, John introduces several themes that carry throughout the Gospel.

Evasive Jesus

When you read about the wedding at Cana last week, you might have thought Jesus's response to His mother was a little cold and odd:

> "What has this concern of yours to do with me, woman?"
> Jesus asked. "My hour has not yet come."
> **JOHN 2:4**

Similar statements occur in 7:6,8,30; 8:20. Because of misconceptions about the coming Messiah, Jesus chose not to reveal Himself openly because "His hour had not come." In other words, It was not time for Jesus's full identity to be known by all people—that would come at the cross.

John portrays Jesus as the "elusive Christ" via Jesus's pattern of occasional withdrawal (see 7:6-9; 10:40-41; 11:56-57), His realism about people's true motives (see 2:23-25), and His ability to elude His opponents when charged with blasphemy (see 7:44; 8:59; 10:39). Jesus remained elusive until His time finally arrived (see 12:23,27; 13:1; 16:32; 17:1).

Jesus Lifted Up

Jesus's conversation with Nicodemus contains the first of three "lifted up" sayings in John (see 3:14; 8:28; 12:32). All three speak of the future "lifting up" of the Son of Man in double meaning (possibly inspired by the language of Isaiah 52:13). The reference in this verse invokes Moses's lifting up of a serpent in the wilderness so that everyone who had been bitten by a poisonous snake and looked at the serpent in faith was healed (see Numbers 21:8-9). The third and final "lifted up" saying (John 12:32) emphasizes that the lifting up of the Son of Man refers to Jesus's crucifixion (see 12:33 and the similar reference to Peter's martyrdom in 21:19).[3]

JOHN 3:22-36

JESUS AND JOHN THE BAPTIST

²² After this, Jesus and his disciples went to the Judean countryside, where he spent time with them and baptized.

²³ John also was baptizing in Aenon near Salim, because there was plenty of water there. People were coming and being baptized, ²⁴ since John had not yet been thrown into prison.

²⁵ Then a dispute arose between John's disciples and a Jew about purification. ²⁶ So they came to John and told him, "Rabbi, the one you testified about, and who was with you across the Jordan, is baptizing — and everyone is going to him."

²⁷ John responded, "No one can receive anything unless it has been given to him from heaven. ²⁸ You yourselves can testify that I said, 'I am not the Messiah, but I've been sent ahead of him.' ²⁹ He who has the bride is the groom. But the groom's friend, who stands by and listens for him, rejoices greatly at the groom's voice. So this joy of mine is complete. ³⁰ He must increase, but I must decrease."

THE ONE FROM HEAVEN

³¹ The one who comes from above is above all. The one who is from the earth is earthly and speaks in earthly terms. The one who comes from heaven is above all. ³² He testifies to what he has seen and heard, and yet no one accepts his testimony. ³³ The one who has accepted his testimony has affirmed that God is true. ³⁴ For the one whom God sent speaks God's words, since he gives the Spirit without measure. ³⁵ The Father loves the Son and has given all things into his hands. ³⁶ The one who believes in the Son has eternal life, but the one who rejects the Son will not see life; instead, the wrath of God remains on him.

YOU EXIST FOR SOMEONE ELSE

In the first century when Jesus ministered on earth, it was common for master teachers, or rabbis, to have a group of disciples who followed them around and learned from them. We see this pattern with Jesus and His disciples, as well as with John the Baptist and his disciples.

In these verses John the Baptist's disciples came to him with an issue: people were leaving John the Baptist and following Jesus. This concerned them because Jews at the time held the rabbi that they followed in highest esteem. And those rabbis held their followers in high esteem, often transferring wealth and status to their disciples. When these disciples saw some of John the Baptist's followers link with Jesus and His teachings, they were ready to defend their rabbi.

But John the Baptist took this opportunity to teach them, and us, about who Jesus is and what true humility looks like. He said Jesus was the groom and he was simply a friend of the groom. John was ready for his influence, status, and even his disciples to leave him if that's what it took to help others see who Jesus is. John the Baptist understood his place in the story of Scripture. He only existed to point people to someone else. He had no desire to reign on a throne of man-made influence. He was ready to decrease so that Jesus would increase.

John resisted the temptation to build himself up. In a time with platforms, followers, and influencers, we can look back to a man who rejected all of that to find himself in Jesus. He understood that anything Jesus had to offer was better than anything status and followers could give him. There's only one King—the One in whom our belief constitutes a gift of the "Spirit without measure" (John 3:34).

Jesus invites us to live for Him
and die to ourselves.

REFLECTIONS

What did John the Baptist mean in John 3:29 when he said, "This joy of mine is complete"?

Where do you feel the draw and pull of influence?

Confess to God a time when you've sought glory and recognition in life rather than pointing the glory back to God.

JOHN 4:1-26

JESUS AND THE SAMARITAN WOMAN

4 When Jesus learned that the Pharisees had heard he was making and baptizing more disciples than John ² (though Jesus himself was not baptizing, but his disciples were), ³ he left Judea and went again to Galilee. ⁴ He had to travel through Samaria; ⁵ so he came to a town of Samaria called Sychar near the property that Jacob had given his son Joseph. ⁶ Jacob's well was there, and Jesus, worn out from his journey, sat down at the well. It was about noon.

⁷ A woman of Samaria came to draw water.

"Give me a drink," Jesus said to her, ⁸ because his disciples had gone into town to buy food.

⁹ "How is it that you, a Jew, ask for a drink from me, a Samaritan woman?" she asked him. For Jews do not associate with Samaritans.

¹⁰ Jesus answered, "If you knew the gift of God, and who is saying to you, 'Give me a drink,' you would ask him, and he would give you living water."

¹¹ "Sir," said the woman, "you don't even have a bucket, and the well is deep. So where do you get this 'living water'? ¹² You aren't greater than our father Jacob, are you? He gave us the well and drank from it himself, as did his sons and livestock."

¹³ Jesus said, "Everyone who drinks from this water will get thirsty again. ¹⁴ But whoever drinks from the water that I will give him will never get thirsty again. In fact, the water I will give him will become a well of water springing up in him for eternal life."

¹⁵ "Sir," the woman said to him, "give me this water so that I won't get thirsty and come here to draw water."

¹⁶ "Go call your husband," he told her, "and come back here."

¹⁷ "I don't have a husband," she answered.

"You have correctly said, 'I don't have a husband,'" Jesus said. ¹⁸ "For you've had five husbands, and the man you now have is not your husband. What you have said is true."

¹⁹ "Sir," the woman replied, "I see that you are a prophet. ²⁰ Our ancestors worshiped on this mountain, but you Jews say that the place to worship is in Jerusalem."

²¹ Jesus told her, "Believe me, woman, an hour is coming when you will worship the Father neither on this mountain nor in Jerusalem. ²² You Samaritans worship what you do not know. We worship what we do know, because salvation is from the Jews. ²³ But an hour is coming, and is now here, when the true worshipers will worship the Father in Spirit and in truth. Yes, the Father wants such people to worship him. ²⁴ God is spirit, and those who worship him must worship in Spirit and in truth."

²⁵ The woman said to him, "I know that the Messiah is coming" (who is called Christ). "When he comes, he will explain everything to us."

²⁶ Jesus told her, "I, the one speaking to you, am he."

NEVER THIRST

Have you ever zoned out in a conversation, and when you refocus, you realize you've missed a key detail? You try to catch up, but nobody's giving you the context clues you need to discover what you've missed. It's confusing and frustrating, isn't it? But it's so wonderful when your friend leans over and whispers to you the line you missed that fills in all the gaps!

That's what's going on here with Jesus and the woman at the well. Jesus traveled through Sychar in Samaria and stopped by a well to drink. At noon on a hot day, most of the town would be indoors. But not the Samaritan woman. The fact that Jesus talked directly with her put Him in serious violation of the cultural norms of the day. At that time, men wouldn't talk publicly to a woman like this, nor would a Jew talk with a Samaritan. But the point of this conversation isn't Jesus's willingness to break cultural norms; it's His willingness to meet our deepest needs with His abundant resources.

She thought they were both in need of water, not realizing Jesus could give her something of much greater value. In this conversation, Jesus used the setting (the well) to start a conversation about her deep spiritual need and revealed yet another aspect of who He is. He's not just a prophet—He's the Messiah, "Who is called Christ" (v. 25).

At first the woman tried to dodge the issue and talk about their cultural and theological differences. She almost missed that the King was right in front of her! But Jesus led her to back to Himself, like He so often does with us.

Just like in a conversation when your friend lets you in on what you missed, Jesus told the woman that He was the long-awaited Messiah, that He would explain everything to her, and that He was the One she'd been looking for. There is nothing any of us need more than this conversation.

He invites us to satisfy our
souls with living water.

REFLECTIONS

What arguments did the woman use as Jesus continued to press in?

What helped this woman see Jesus for who He is? What have you noticed about Jesus lately or through this study?

INSIGHT

After the fall of the Northern Kingdom of Israel to the Assyrians, many Israelites were led away in slavery to their conquerers. However, some stayed back and married foreign residents in Assyria. These intermarried people, half-Jewish and half-non-Jewish, became known as Samaritans. There was a contentious rift between Jews and Samaritans surrounding worship practices. Jesus would destroy this dividing wall through His life and death, proving what He claimed in John 4:23-24: worship isn't about the location—it's about the heart.

JOHN 4:27-42

THE RIPENED HARVEST

27 Just then his disciples arrived, and they were amazed that he was talking with a woman. Yet no one said, "What do you want?" or "Why are you talking with her?"

28 Then the woman left her water jar, went into town, and told the people, 29 "Come, see a man who told me everything I ever did. Could this be the Messiah?" 30 They left the town and made their way to him.

31 In the meantime the disciples kept urging him, "Rabbi, eat something."

32 But he said, "I have food to eat that you don't know about."

33 The disciples said to one another, "Could someone have brought him something to eat?"

34 "My food is to do the will of him who sent me and to finish his work," Jesus told them. 35 "Don't you say, 'There are still four more months, and then comes the harvest'? Listen to what I'm telling you: Open your eyes and look at the fields, because they are ready for harvest. 36 The reaper is already receiving pay and gathering fruit for eternal life, so that the sower and reaper can rejoice together. 37 For in this case the saying is true: 'One sows and another reaps.' 38 I sent you to reap what you didn't labor for; others have labored, and you have benefited from their labor."

THE SAVIOR OF THE WORLD

39 Now many Samaritans from that town believed in him because of what the woman said when she testified, "He told me everything I ever did." 40 So when the Samaritans came to him, they asked him to stay with them, and he stayed there two days. 41 Many more believed because of what he said. 42 And they told the woman, "We no longer believe because of what you said, since we have heard for ourselves and know that this really is the Savior of the world."

COME SEE

What if something wonderful happened to you, but you didn't have anyone to tell? It likely wouldn't feel as satisfying. In many cases, for joy to be complete it must be shared. This is why many marketing and ad campaigns depend on word of mouth. They're expecting people who have good experiences to share them. That's what the Samaritan woman did after speaking with Jesus.

The woman left her water jar—the reason she came to the well in the first place— and went to tell everyone in town what happened. She appears to have been rather indiscriminate with her news too. She didn't cast a small net with a close group of friends, she told every person she saw.

Her belief couldn't be held in, and apparently, it was convincing. Many people left the town and made their way to Jesus. What they found was so compelling that they ask Jesus to stay with them, and He did—for two more days. Then Scripture says, "Many more believed because of what he said" (v. 41).

But that wasn't the only conversation happening in this passage. John also gives us an inside look at Jesus with His disciples. Here He told them that the fields were ready for the harvest. In other words, people were ready to believe in Him.

Amazingly, this was happening with the Samaritans while Jesus was teaching His disciples. For the first time in John's Gospel, the good news was expanding beyond the Jews to the surrounding people. While Jesus would be rejected and rebuffed by the religious leaders of His own people, these Samaritans were able to receive Him and recognize that He truly is the "Savior of the world" (v. 42).

It is just as unlikely that the gospel would come to us. We are no more deserving than the Samaritans, yet if you're reading this book, the gospel has come to you. The question for us all is, *What will we do with it?*

Those who find Him share Him.

REFLECTIONS

Why were the disciples still confused about Jesus's words? What does the Samaritan belief in Jesus teach us about Him?

How does sharing our joy complete our joy?

What are you learning about Jesus that is too good to keep to yourself? Who might you tell, even if it's another Christian?

JOHN 4:43-54

A GALILEAN WELCOME

[43] After two days he left there for Galilee. [44] (Jesus himself had testified that a prophet has no honor in his own country.) [45] When they entered Galilee, the Galileans welcomed him because they had seen everything he did in Jerusalem during the festival. For they also had gone to the festival.

THE SECOND SIGN: HEALING AN OFFICIAL'S SON

[46] He went again to Cana of Galilee, where he had turned the water into wine. There was a certain royal official whose son was ill at Capernaum. [47] When this man heard that Jesus had come from Judea into Galilee, he went to him and pleaded with him to come down and heal his son, since he was about to die.

[48] Jesus told him, "Unless you people see signs and wonders, you will not believe."

[49] "Sir," the official said to him, "come down before my boy dies."

[50] "Go," Jesus told him, "your son will live." The man believed what Jesus said to him and departed.

[51] While he was still going down, his servants met him saying that his boy was alive. [52] He asked them at what time he got better. "Yesterday at one in the afternoon the fever left him," they answered. [53] The father realized this was the very hour at which Jesus had told him, "Your son will live." So he himself believed, along with his whole household.

[54] Now this was also the second sign Jesus performed after he came from Judea to Galilee.

THE SECOND SIGN

Here we see the second sign John highlights to reveal who Jesus is: the healing of the royal official's son.

Jesus returned to the region where He grew up, Galilee (see Luke 2:39-40). There He encountered a royal official whose son was sick in Capernaum, which was about twenty miles away. This man approached Jesus to request healing for his son.

Like the previous encounter with the Samaritan woman, John made intentional contrasts. The story contrasts two different responses to Jesus: the Jews from Galilee and the royal official. Jesus rebuked the Jews, who were only seeking Him for "signs and wonders" (John 4:48). They were enamored by His abilities, yet their lives were unchanged.

But the royal official's response was different. Though he was rebuffed by Jesus, the official continued to implore, and in an act of mercy, Jesus granted the request. The boy was healed at the very moment Jesus said he would live. The official believed in faith that Jesus had the power to heal his son, and Jesus honored his faith. But the official's belief was more than lip service. When Jesus told him to go home, he went, believing Jesus had done what He said He would.

The official heard Jesus's words and obeyed, trusting that what Jesus says is good and right. In contrast, the Jews in Galilee needed to see Jesus perform signs and wonders in order to believe.

This sign, like the first that we read about (Jesus turning water into wine) is more than just a miracle, though it surely is that. It's a sign pointing to a greater reality, that this Man, Jesus, was truly God Himself, and He had power over life and death.

Jesus alone holds the
power of life and death.

REFLECTIONS

What stands out to you about the faith of the royal official in this passage?

Read James 1:19-27. Compare the Jews' response to Jesus with the royal official's response to Jesus.

What is Jesus asking you to trust Him with today? Where are you seeking a sign when you should simply believe?

"For God loved the world in this way: He gave his one and only Son, so that everyone who believes in him will not perish but have eternal life."

JOHN 3:16

REFLECTION

Use these questions for personal reflection or group discussion on John 3:1–4:54.

What stuck out to you most in this week's reading? What surprised you? Confused you?

What does this week's Scripture teach you about God and His character?

What does this week's Scripture teach you about humanity and our need for grace?

How does this week's Scripture point you to Jesus?

Where do you need a miracle right now? Based on the Scriptures you read this week, how can you prepare your heart for what Jesus might do in your life?

PRAY

We serve the same God today who worked the miracles we've read about. Pray for yourself or someone you know who needs a miracle. Ask God to give you eyes to see the miracle and ask Him to strengthen your faith through it.

WEEK 3

I AM WORKING ALSO

Jesus set about
His Father's work.

In contrast to the intimate and measured conversations observed last week, this week's reading features Jesus in action—performing miracles, attesting to His identity, having more contentious conversations, and challenging unbelief.

This week begins what is known as the Festival Cycle in John because the activity is organized around Jesus's interactions around the various Jewish celebrations and festivals.

Noticing these patterns and features built into the Scriptures give a great appreciation for what the authors were doing and helps us connect the event to real times and places.

Jesus performed many signs and had many conversations asking all who saw to believe. These words are as much for us as they were for the original participants to lean in and drink deeply.

JOHN 5:1-16

THE THIRD SIGN: HEALING THE SICK

5 After this, a Jewish festival took place, and Jesus went up to Jerusalem. [2] By the Sheep Gate in Jerusalem there is a pool, called Bethesda in Aramaic, which has five colonnades. [3] Within these lay a large number of the disabled—blind, lame, and paralyzed. *

[5] One man was there who had been disabled for thirty-eight years. [6] When Jesus saw him lying there and realized he had already been there a long time, he said to him, "Do you want to get well?"

[7] "Sir," the disabled man answered, "I have no one to put me into the pool when the water is stirred up, but while I'm coming, someone goes down ahead of me."

[8] "Get up," Jesus told him, "pick up your mat and walk." [9] Instantly the man got well, picked up his mat, and started to walk.

Now that day was the Sabbath, [10] and so the Jews said to the man who had been healed, "This is the Sabbath. The law prohibits you from picking up your mat."

[11] He replied, "The man who made me well told me, 'Pick up your mat and walk.'"

[12] "Who is this man who told you, 'Pick up your mat and walk'?" they asked. [13] But the man who was healed did not know who it was, because Jesus had slipped away into the crowd that was there.

[14] After this, Jesus found him in the temple and said to him, "See, you are well. Do not sin anymore, so that something worse doesn't happen to you." [15] The man went and reported to the Jews that it was Jesus who had made him well. [16] Therefore, the Jews began persecuting Jesus because he was doing these things on the Sabbath.

THE THIRD SIGN

In his book, *Poor Richard's Almanac*, Benjamin Franklin said, "God helps them that help themselves,"[4] a phrase which has remained popular with many people to this day. Some even think this is a quote from the Bible. Yet today's Scripture reading proves that Franklin was wrong. In fact, what we learn is that Jesus helps those who can't help themselves.

Jesus traveled to the Pool of Bethesda, which was a place rumored to have miraculous healing powers. Those John called "the disabled" (v. 3) flocked there in search of healing. Most people would've walked by without giving these people a second glance, but Jesus took the time to single one of these men out. He saw the need and sought to address it.

In an instant, Jesus overcame thirty-eight years of suffering. The severity of the man's disability was of no consequence to Jesus. We sometimes grow hopeless when someone's sickness lingers, especially if they're spiritually sick. Yet by helping a man who could not help himself, Jesus proved that He can overcome years of suffering in a single moment.

Instead of receiving this obvious miracle with awe and reverence, the Jewish leaders accused the man of lawbreaking for picking up his mat. The man later found Jesus and reported Him to the Jewish authorities. Based on his report, the Jewish leaders "began persecuting Jesus because he was doing these things on the Sabbath" (v. 16). Jesus and the work He was doing didn't fit into their box, and instead of changing that box, they persecuted Him.

The miracle of this third sign is found in each and every one of our helpless states. We are unable to save ourselves, so Jesus intervened and offers us a new life—something only the God of the universe is able to do.

But sometimes a miracle is not enough. The authorities saw the healing firsthand and the disabled man experienced it in his body, and there was still disbelief.

It is possible to see and experience
Jesus and still miss Him.

REFLECTIONS

How did the Jewish leaders "miss" Jesus even though they witnessed His healing power?

How do you miss Jesus even when you've experienced His healing?

Where do you feel weakest right now? How is that an area of your life where you can allow the power of God to shine in and through you (see 2 Corinthians 12:10)?

INSIGHTS

Close to the Sheep Gate, where sheep were brought in to the market, was a pool (likely two pools) where people would gather for healing. "Bethesda may mean 'house of mercy,' a fitting term given the desperate state of the people who lay there hoping for a miraculous cure."[5]

FESTIVALS *in* JOHN

John chapters 5–10 are known as the Festival Cycle because much of the narrative involved conversations in and around Jewish ceremonial festivals. These chapters feature escalating controversy between Jesus and Jewish authorities. John's original audience would've been understood these festivals and their significance immediately. John was trying to show His audience that Jesus was the fulfillment of these Jewish feasts, but to make that connection, modern readers need a little help.

The Unnamed Festival

After this, a Jewish festival took place, and Jesus went up to Jerusalem.
JOHN 5:1

This first unnamed festival was likely Passover or the Festival of Shelters. "After this" signals a shift in time in John. These events were like several months to a year after the events in chapter 4. This provided an occasion for Jesus to defend His ministry and enumerate evidences for His identity.

The Festival of Unleavened Bread

Now the Passover, a Jewish festival, was near.
JOHN 6:4

Passover is the backdrop for Jesus's feeding of the five thousand and His teaching on being the Bread of Life. This is the second Passover mentioned in John. The Passover is the first and most important annual Jewish festival. It commemorated the final plague on Egypt when the firstborn of the Egyptians died and the Israelites were spared because of the blood smeared on their doorposts (see Exodus 12:11,21,27,43,48).

The Passover was also called the feast of unleavened bread (see Exodus 23:15; Deuteronomy 16:16) because only unleavened bread was eaten during the seven days immediately following Passover (see Exodus 12:15-20; 13:6-8; Deuteronomy 16:3-8). Unleavened bread reflected the fact that the people had no time to put leaven in their bread before their hasty departure from Egypt. It was also apparently connected to the barley harvest (see Leviticus 23:4-14).[6]

The Festival of Shelters

The Jewish Festival of Shelters, was near.
JOHN 7:2

The fourth annual festival was the Festival of Shelters, or booths or tabernacles (see 2 Chronicles 8:13; Ezra 3:4; Zechariah 14:16). It celebrated the Lord's provision for the harvest. Its celebrated the ingathering of the labor of the field (see Exodus 23:16), the fruit of the earth (see Leviticus 23:39), the ingathering of the threshing floor and winepress (see Deuteronomy 16:13), and the dwelling in shelters, which were to be joyful reminders to Israel (see Leviticus 23:41; Deuteronomy 16:14). The "shelter" in Scripture is an image of protection, preservation, and shelter from heat and storm (see Psalm 27:5; 31:20; Isaiah 4:6). The rejoicing community included family, servants, widows, orphans, Levites, and sojourners (see Deuteronomy 16:13–15).[7]

John was teaching that Jesus is our ultimate provision and shelter—whether He was recognized or not.

The Festival of Dedication

Then the Festival of Dedication took place in Jerusalem, and it was winter.
JOHN 10:22

Also called the Festival of Lights (or modernly, Hanukkah), the origins go back to the time between the Old Testament and New Testament when a group of Jewish fighters known as the Macabees overthrew an oppressive government. This festival celebrated the rededication of the temple. When the Jews returned to the temple, they could only find one jar of oil that hadn't been corrupted, and that oil miraculously lasted for eight days when it should've only lasted for one. This celebration is a reminder that darkness may last for the night, but joy comes in the morning!

JOHN 5:17-30

HONORING THE FATHER AND THE SON

[17] Jesus responded to them, "My Father is still working, and I am working also." [18] This is why the Jews began trying all the more to kill him: Not only was he breaking the Sabbath, but he was even calling God his own Father, making himself equal to God.

[19] Jesus replied, "Truly I tell you, the Son is not able to do anything on his own, but only what he sees the Father doing. For whatever the Father does, the Son likewise does these things. [20] For the Father loves the Son and shows him everything he is doing, and he will show him greater works than these so that you will be amazed. [21] And just as the Father raises the dead and gives them life, so the Son also gives life to whom he wants. [22] The Father, in fact, judges no one but has given all judgment to the Son, [23] so that all people may honor the Son just as they honor the Father. Anyone who does not honor the Son does not honor the Father who sent him.

LIFE AND JUDGMENT

[24] "Truly I tell you, anyone who hears my word and believes him who sent me has eternal life and will not come under judgment but has passed from death to life.

[25] "Truly I tell you, an hour is coming, and is now here, when the dead will hear the voice of the Son of God, and those who hear will live. [26] For just as the Father has life in himself, so also he has granted to the Son to have life in himself. [27] And he has granted him the right to pass judgment, because he is the Son of Man. [28] Do not be amazed at this, because a time is coming when all who are in the graves will hear his voice [29] and come out — those who have done good things, to the resurrection of life, but those who have done wicked things, to the resurrection of condemnation.

[30] "I can do nothing on my own. I judge only as I hear, and my judgment is just, because I do not seek my own will, but the will of him who sent me."

NOTHING ON MY OWN

Have you ever seen magicians reveal just how they did a particular trick? At first glance, it's fun to be let in on the secret. But then you realize there's an explanation, and it's usually simple. The allure and the mystery leave when you realize what appeared to be magic was just a trick.

These verses continue a conversation that started on day 15. The Jewish leaders continued to go after Jesus about His miracles. They were trying to figure out what the trick was. Jesus was eager to tell them, "There is no trick." Jesus is no street magician letting the crowd in on a game; He is the Son of Man who has come to do the works of His Father.

He explicitly revealed that He is the "Son of Man," a reference to a prophecy from the book of Daniel (7:13-14). In doing so, Jesus fulfilled a prophecy and put Himself on a level playing field with God the Father. That's the purpose of all these miracles—they point to Jesus's unique identity as the Son of God. People observing the first three signs Jesus performed could've deduced where Jesus's power came from, but now there was no denying it.

In the passage yesterday, Jesus addressed spiritual sickness; here He claimed to be able to address spiritual sickness and death. He claimed to hold the key to eternal judgment and offered entry to all who believe in Him. With these words, He was claiming power that only belongs to God. If the signs weren't clear, Jesus confessed with His mouth what many were seeing and coming to believe: He is the Son of God.

And those who hear these words from Jesus and believe them pass from death to life through the power of the Son. He does nothing on His own—all His work points back to the Father.

All Jesus's works point back to the Father.

REFLECTIONS

Why should we lean in and listen when Jesus explains to us why He performs the miracles He does?

What do His answers reveal to us about who He is and what He is like?

Jesus's words grant life in the here and now, not just for eternity. How will you allow Jesus's words to shape you today? To help you pass from death to life?

JOHN 5:31-47

WITNESSES TO JESUS

³¹ "If I testify about myself, my testimony is not true. ³² There is another who testi-fies about me, and I know that the testimony he gives about me is true. ³³ You sent messengers to John, and he testified to the truth. ³⁴ I don't receive human testimony, but I say these things so that you may be saved. ³⁵ John was a burning and shining lamp, and you were willing to rejoice for a while in his light.

³⁶ "But I have a greater testimony than John's because of the works that the Father has given me to accomplish. These very works I am doing testify about me that the Father has sent me. ³⁷ The Father who sent me has himself testified about me. You have not heard his voice at any time, and you haven't seen his form. ³⁸ You don't have his word residing in you, because you don't believe the one he sent. ³⁹ You pore over the Scriptures because you think you have eternal life in them, and yet they testify about me. ⁴⁰ But you are not willing to come to me so that you may have life.

⁴¹ "I do not accept glory from people, ⁴² but I know you — that you have no love for God within you. ⁴³ I have come in my Father's name, and yet you don't accept me. If someone else comes in his own name, you will accept him. ⁴⁴ How can you believe, since you accept glory from one another but don't seek the glory that comes from the only God? ⁴⁵ Do not think that I will accuse you to the Father. Your accuser is Moses, on whom you have set your hope. ⁴⁶ For if you believed Moses, you would believe me, because he wrote about me. ⁴⁷ But if you don't believe what he wrote, how will you believe my words?"

WITNESSES

In a court of law, it's appropriate for you to defend yourself, but by itself, your defense isn't likely to sway a judge to rule in your favor. You need the testimony of a witness. This is what Jesus appealed to in order to verify His claim that He's the Son of God. This is important because the Old Testament law said, "A fact must be established by the testimony of two or three witnesses" (Deuteronomy 19:15). Jesus went over and above that law to illuminate and prove His true identity.

Jesus's identity was verified by John the Baptist, a prophet respected among the Jews. Plus, Jesus's own works served as a witness to His identity because they were clearly from God. That was the point of His signs. Next, God the Father testified about Jesus, yet the Jewish leaders would not accept this because of their unbelief (see v. 38). And the Scriptures themselves, particularly the writings of Moses, point to Jesus too.

Though the Jewish leaders poured over their Bibles, they did not let the truth affect their hearts. They failed to see that every word they read pointed to the Man standing in front of them.

But to the those who don't want to believe, no proof is enough. Evidence alone can't help someone see the truth about Jesus. Our hearts have to be open and receptive to His work.

It's possible to see Jesus, hear from Jesus, and experience Jesus and still miss Him. People in the first century missed it, and we miss it today, but the key to finding Him is simple: open up the Scriptures, like you're doing right now, read about Him, and believe in Him.

The signs and witnesses all stack up, validating that Jesus is exactly who He claimed to be.

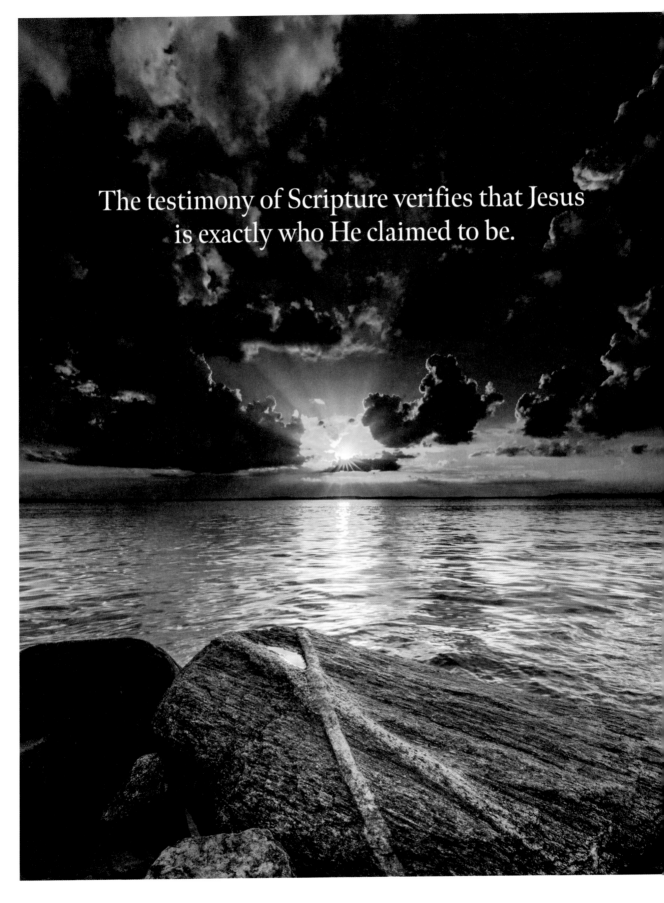

The testimony of Scripture verifies that Jesus is exactly who He claimed to be.

REFLECTIONS

Why is it necessary to have witnesses?

What do you think the holdup was for the Jewish leaders who refused to believe in Jesus? How does our culture experience that holdup today?

How does this passage change the way we engage with the Scriptures?

CONNECTING THE STORY

Jesus was the fulfillment of Moses, who led his people through the exodus from Egypt; Jesus would soon lead His people through the second exodus: from death itself. Moses wandered in the dessert for forty years, yet ultimately failed to enter the promised land. Jesus was tempted in the desert for forty days and passed that test. In total, Jesus claimed five witnesses, which is important because the Old Testament law said, "A fact must be established by the testimony of two or three witnesses" (Deuteronomy 19:15). Jesus went over and above that law to illuminate and prove His true identity.

JOHN 6:1-15

THE FOURTH SIGN: FEEDING OF THE FIVE THOUSAND

6 After this, Jesus crossed the Sea of Galilee (or Tiberias). [2] A huge crowd was following him because they saw the signs that he was performing by healing the sick. [3] Jesus went up a mountain and sat down there with his disciples.

[4] Now the Passover, a Jewish festival, was near. [5] So when Jesus looked up and noticed a huge crowd coming toward him, he asked Philip, "Where will we buy bread so that these people can eat?" [6] He asked this to test him, for he himself knew what he was going to do.

[7] Philip answered him, "Two hundred denarii worth of bread wouldn't be enough for each of them to have a little."

[8] One of his disciples, Andrew, Simon Peter's brother, said to him, [9] "There's a boy here who has five barley loaves and two fish — but what are they for so many?"

[10] Jesus said, "Have the people sit down."

There was plenty of grass in that place; so they sat down. The men numbered about five thousand. [11] Then Jesus took the loaves, and after giving thanks he distributed them to those who were seated — so also with the fish, as much as they wanted.

[12] When they were full, he told his disciples, "Collect the leftovers so that nothing is wasted." [13] So they collected them and filled twelve baskets with the pieces from the five barley loaves that were left over by those who had eaten.

[14] When the people saw the sign he had done, they said, "This truly is the Prophet who is to come into the world."

[15] Therefore, when Jesus realized that they were about to come and take him by force to make him king, he withdrew again to the mountain by himself.

THE FOURTH SIGN

As Jesus's fame spread throughout the region, He amassed a following. Crowds came, eager to experience one of the miracles or healings they had heard so much about. Jesus saw the crowd and asked Philip what seemed to be a natural question, "What are they going to eat?"

Five thousand men were present, but this meant many more were there, because the number didn't include women and children. There were far more people than provisions. To feed this large group of people would cost more than six month's wages. Yet physical resources are never a limitation for Jesus. Jesus in His mercy and compassion fed everyone "as much as they wanted" (John 6:11).

Jesus is not limited by our doubts or by our resources. He can take what we offer and turn it into more than we could imagine. There were twelve baskets left over both because that's how many apostles where were and because there were twelve tribes of Israel.

This act from Jesus was more than a way to feed a crowd; it was meant to forge a connection to other parts of the story. This sign also echoes the way God fed the Israelites in the wilderness as they wandered (see Exodus 16). The conversation in the rest of chapter 6 with flesh this out further.

However, like Jesus's other signs, the crowds here misinterpreted it. They recognized Jesus was a prophet, but they wanted for Jesus things Jesus did want or expect for Himself. They expected their Prophet to be a king, ruling politically and militarily like a general who would lead the Israelites to freedom from the Romans. Many of us expect Jesus to be something He's not too.

They thought too small of what their Prophet could do. Jesus's power and miracles are always given to point back to God, testify about His identity, and give grace to all who experience them.

Jesus takes what we offer and multiplies it for His purpose.

REFLECTIONS

Why would Jesus ask a question to test Philip?

How has Jesus provided for you in gracious and extravagant ways?

How does this story and this sign change the way you pray?

CONNECTING THE STORY

"After this" (John 6:1) at the beginning of these verses signals a time shift. As much as half a year may have passed since the conversations in chapter 5. The time of this event was close to Passover and people were flocking to Jerusalem, which would explain the large crowd following Jesus.

JOHN 6:16-21

THE FIFTH SIGN: WALKING ON WATER

[16] When evening came, his disciples went down to the sea, [17] got into a boat, and started across the sea to Capernaum. Darkness had already set in, but Jesus had not yet come to them. [18] A high wind arose, and the sea began to churn. [19] After they had rowed about three or four miles, they saw Jesus walking on the sea. He was coming near the boat, and they were afraid. [20] But he said to them, "It is I. Don't be afraid." [21] Then they were willing to take him on board, and at once the boat was at the shore where they were heading.

WALKING ON WATER

Unlike the other signs, this sign was done for the benefit of Jesus's disciples. They were alone on a boat (see Matthew 14:22). The watchful eyes of the crowd were left behind for this intimate work.

After the events of the previous verses, Jesus sought time alone to pray while He sent the disciples across the lake to Capernaum (see Matthew 14:23). After they'd rowed about three or four miles, a storm popped up. This would've been a route familiar to the disciples, yet this storm stalled them out. The waves were crashing all around them, and the disciples saw a man walking toward them. Naturally, they were afraid.

Then Jesus called out, announcing that it was Him. Interestingly, the language used here and translated "It is I" is a direct connection to the personal name God gave in Exodus 3:14, "I am who I am."

While John is scarce on details, we know from Matthew and Mark that Jesus calmed the storm with the command of His voice and the disciples confessed that He is the Son of God (see Matthew 14:33). However, only John recorded that the boat was immediately on the other side.

Only God Himself has authority over the weather. Only God can immediately move a boat from the middle of a lake to the shore. Jesus's power and authority has no other explanation that fits other than, "This man is God."

Jesus was in charge the whole time, not just when the disciples recognized His authority. And we can trust this in our lives too, knowing no matter what we face, Jesus is in charge. There is nothing outside of His control. What God has belongs to Him. What belongs to Him can be ours through having faith.

Jesus is the powerful Son of God who commands the wind and waves.

REFLECTIONS

Why does it matter that Jesus has control over the natural world?

What relevance does that have for us?

How should this sign encourage you to love and trust Jesus more?

PAUSE & LISTEN

Spend some time reflecting over the week's reading.

"You pore over the Scriptures because
you think you have eternal life in them,
and yet they testify about me."

JOHN 5:39

REFLECTION

Use these questions for personal reflection or group discussion on John 5:1–6:21.

What stuck out to you most in this week's reading? What surprised you? Confused you?

What does this week's Scripture teach you about God and His character?

What does this week's Scripture teach you about humanity and our need for grace?

How does this week's Scripture point you to Jesus?

Where do you currently doubt—or where have you doubted in the past—that Jesus is who He says He is? Which of the signs so far appeals most to your doubts? Why?

PRAY

Thank God for showing us who He is through powerful signs and the testimony of His Word. Ask Him to help us to be people who receive it, believe, and trust Him with our lives.

BELIEVE IN
THE ONE HE SENT

Our questions should
lead us into belief.

Interrogation is a reoccurring theme in the Gospel of John.

Throughout his Gospel, John introduces compelling evidence—testimony of expert witnesses, signs that prove Jesus's identity, and Jesus's own testimony—that Jesus is the Jewish Messiah, the Son of God. One of the ways John accomplished this is by recording the questions people asked about Jesus.

This week's reading features more of these questions than any other section in John. As we read, we come alongside people wrestling with Jesus's identity in real time. Who is this Man? Could He be the Messiah? Who else could do these things? All of these questions are meant to lead us to the conclusion that, yes, Jesus is who He says He is.

He is the only satisfying answer to the deepest questions of our souls.

THE BREAD OF LIFE

22 The next day, the crowd that had stayed on the other side of the sea saw there had been only one boat. They also saw that Jesus had not boarded the boat with his disciples, but that his disciples had gone off alone. 23 Some boats from Tiberias came near the place where they had eaten the bread after the Lord had given thanks. 24 When the crowd saw that neither Jesus nor his disciples were there, they got into the boats and went to Capernaum looking for Jesus. 25 When they found him on the other side of the sea, they said to him, "Rabbi, when did you get here?"

26 Jesus answered, "Truly I tell you, you are looking for me, not because you saw the signs, but because you ate the loaves and were filled. 27 Don't work for the food that perishes but for the food that lasts for eternal life, which the Son of Man will give you, because God the Father has set his seal of approval on him."

28 "What can we do to perform the works of God?" they asked.

29 Jesus replied, "This is the work of God — that you believe in the one he has sent."

30 "What sign, then, are you going to do so that we may see and believe you?" they asked. "What are you going to perform? 31 Our ancestors ate the manna in the wilderness, just as it is written: **He gave them bread from heaven to eat.**"

32 Jesus said to them, "Truly I tell you, Moses didn't give you the bread from heaven, but my Father gives you the true bread from heaven. 33 For the bread of God is the one who comes down from heaven and gives life to the world."

34 Then they said, "Sir, give us this bread always."

35 "I am the bread of life," Jesus told them. "No one who comes to me will ever be hungry, and no one who believes in me will ever be thirsty again. 36 But as I told you, you've seen me, and yet you do not believe. 37 Everyone the Father gives me will come to me, and the one who comes to me I will never cast out. 38 For I have come down from heaven, not to do my own will, but the will of him who sent me. 39 This is the will of him who sent me: that I should lose none of those he has given me but should raise them up on the last day. 40 For this is the will of my Father: that everyone who sees the Son and believes in him will have eternal life, and I will raise him up on the last day."

41 Therefore the Jews started grumbling about him because he said, "I am the bread that came down from heaven." 42 They were saying, "Isn't this Jesus the son of Joseph, whose father and mother we know? How can he now say, 'I have come down from heaven'?"

43 Jesus answered them, "Stop grumbling among yourselves. 44 No one can come to me unless the Father who sent me draws him, and I will raise him up on the last day. 45 It is written in the Prophets: **And they will all be taught by God.** Everyone who has listened to and learned from the Father comes to me — 46 not that anyone has seen the Father except the one who is from God. He has seen the Father.

47 "Truly I tell you, anyone who believes has eternal life. 48 I am the bread of life. 49 Your ancestors ate the manna in the wilderness, and they died. 50 This is the bread that comes down from heaven so that anyone may eat of it and not die. 51 I am the living bread that came down from heaven. If anyone eats of this bread he will live forever. The bread that I will give for the life of the world is my flesh."

52 At that, the Jews argued among themselves, "How can this man give us his flesh to eat?"

53 So Jesus said to them, "Truly I tell you, unless you eat the flesh of the Son of Man and drink his blood, you do not have life in yourselves. 54 The one who eats my flesh and drinks my blood has eternal life, and I will raise him up on the last day, 55 because my flesh is true food and my blood is true drink. 56 The one who eats my flesh and drinks my blood remains in me, and I in him. 57 Just as the living Father sent me and I live because of the Father, so the one who feeds on me will live because of me. 58 This is the bread that came down from heaven; it is not like the manna your ancestors ate — and they died. The one who eats this bread will live forever."

59 He said these things while teaching in the synagogue in Capernaum.

THE BREAD OF LIFE

Think about your favorite vacation you've ever taken. Maybe it was a big road trip. Maybe you had your feet in the sand at the beach, or hiked to the top of a mountain. Maybe you took a plane to some faraway land.

But it's very unlikely that you took a trip to a sign. Families don't drive across the country to park and stare at a road sign. They drive past the sign because signs tell you where to go and what's coming up. They point to something different, something greater and more beautiful. We don't get caught by the sign, we look to where the sign is pointing.

Going back to the feeding of the five thousand, we see that the Jews had grown more and more confused over these signs and their purpose. Jesus corrected them, saying they were not looking for Him because of the signs—they just appreciated that their bellies were filled. In fact, they'd reached the point of wanting Jesus to duplicate His signs, continuing to feed them! They'd missed the point that the Messiah is the Bread of Life who offers eternal life.

Jesus helped them see where the signs were pointing by taking them back to the story of the exodus. When the Jews were wandering in the wilderness, God provided for their needs by giving them manna from heaven. But if you continue reading that story, you'll learn that the manna that came down from heaven ultimately didn't satisfy. Every night it spoiled, and every day they needed more. But the bread Jesus offered would last forever. The people who ate the manna all died, but those who feast on the bread Jesus offers—though they die—will have eternal life.

If you want eternal life, look past the sign to the One who performs it. When we trust Jesus as our Savior, we receive spiritual nourishment that never spoils.

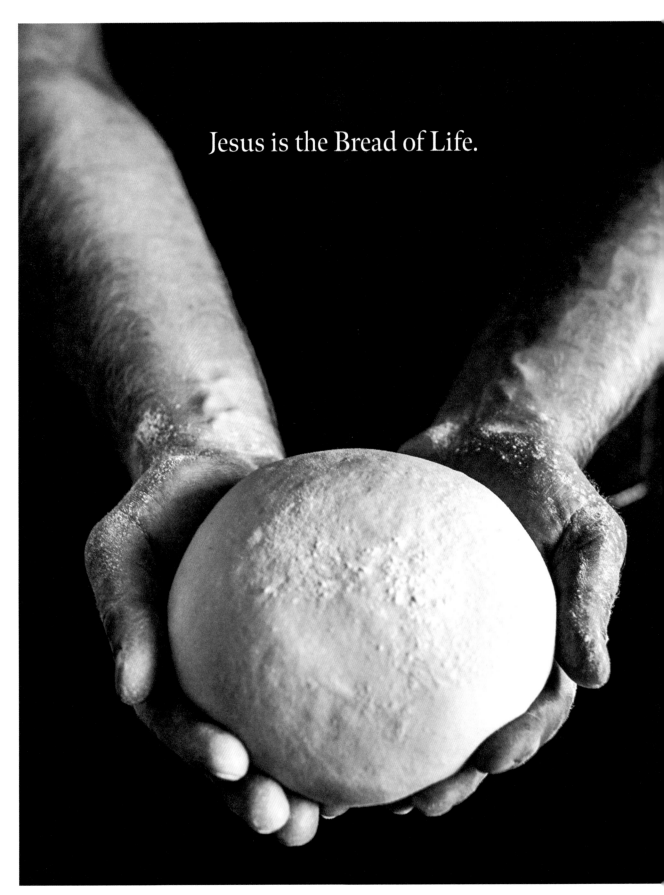

REFLECTIONS

In your own words, compare and contrast Jesus as the Bread of Life with the manna the Israelites ate in the wilderness.

What does the title "Bread of Life" teach us about Jesus?

CONNECTING THE STORY

What did Jesus mean when he talked of eating his flesh and drinking His blood? He was saying people needed to remain—abide, dwell, be present, stay—in Jesus. He is saying that we exist and are sustained by Him and in Him alone. But if you're confused, you're not alone—the people around Jesus were confused too. Some even stopped following Jesus because they didn't understand what He was talking about (see John 6:66). For Jesus, eating was equated with belief. "He promises eternal life to those who believe in him. Believe what? Believe that his death—the breaking of his body and spilling of his blood—pays in full the penalty for our sin, and that his perfect righteousness is freely given to us in exchange for our unrighteousness. . . . This is why he instituted the Lord's Supper: he did not want us to forget the very core of what we believe."[8]

JOHN 6:60-71

MANY DISCIPLES DESERT JESUS

⁶⁰ Therefore, when many of his disciples heard this, they said, "This teaching is hard. Who can accept it?"

⁶¹ Jesus, knowing in himself that his disciples were grumbling about this, asked them, "Does this offend you? ⁶² Then what if you were to observe the Son of Man ascending to where he was before? ⁶³ The Spirit is the one who gives life. The flesh doesn't help at all. The words that I have spoken to you are spirit and are life. ⁶⁴ But there are some among you who don't believe." (For Jesus knew from the beginning those who did not believe and the one who would betray him.) ⁶⁵ He said, "This is why I told you that no one can come to me unless it is granted to him by the Father."

⁶⁶ From that moment many of his disciples turned back and no longer accompanied him. ⁶⁷ So Jesus said to the Twelve, "You don't want to go away too, do you?"

⁶⁸ Simon Peter answered, "Lord, to whom will we go? You have the words of eternal life. ⁶⁹ We have come to believe and know that you are the Holy One of God."

⁷⁰ Jesus replied to them, "Didn't I choose you, the Twelve? Yet one of you is a devil." ⁷¹ He was referring to Judas, Simon Iscariot's son, one of the Twelve, because he was going to betray him.

.

SUPERNATURAL BELIEF

In Jesus's earthly ministry He served three broad audiences: crowds—the large gatherings of people with whom Jesus interacts; the disciples—a smaller group that believed in and started to follow Jesus; and the twelve—the group of apostles Jesus specifically called and empowered for ministry. These verses include the last two groups.

Some of the larger group of disciples were struggling to believe Jesus's teachings. The teaching in yesterday's reading was too difficult for them. They hadn't fully counted the cost and didn't completely believe. Maybe the disciples had begun to listen to the doubting voices of the crowds of Jewish leaders. Or maybe they had personal reasons for not fully believing Jesus was who He claimed He was. Whatever the reason, the truth is that they'd witnessed the signs and heard the teaching, but Jesus as the Messiah still didn't fit their paradigm.

Yet Peter, the most consistently outspoken disciple, declared correctly for the first time that Jesus is the true, Holy One of God. While Peter might not have understood all of what that meant, he recognized that Jesus had something better that could not be found anywhere else. No one compared to Jesus.

What seems to be a meager belief is enough. Maybe like Jesus's disciples, you've witnessed the signs and miracles of Jesus but have experienced seasons plagued by disbelief. If so, you're human. But if you can now declare along with Peter that Jesus is the Holy One of God, then know that this declaration is a work of God in your life. Jesus told the disciples, "No one can come to me unless it is granted to him by the Father" (v. 65). Seeing and believing that Jesus is the Son of God is supernatural; it comes to us as a gift from God. That's why we can hold on to it when everything around us is shaken. Though you will have tough days and doubts can still creep in (see John 16:33), take hope in the truth that no one can snatch you out of Jesus's hand (see John 10:28-30).

Jesus offers more than anyone
or anything else could give us.

REFLECTIONS

Why would Jesus ask the disciples if they planned to walk away too? What might He have been trying to teach them?

Do you know someone who once believed but now has walked away? How does this passage inform the way you pray for them?

How can you use this passage to help dispel the doubt in your life or someone else's life this week?

JOHN 7:1-24

THE UNBELIEF OF JESUS'S BROTHERS

7 After this, Jesus traveled in Galilee, since he did not want to travel in Judea because the Jews were trying to kill him. ² The Jewish Festival of Shelters was near. ³ So his brothers said to him, "Leave here and go to Judea so that your disciples can see your works that you are doing. ⁴ For no one does anything in secret while he's seeking public recognition. If you do these things, show yourself to the world." ⁵ (For not even his brothers believed in him.)

⁶ Jesus told them, "My time has not yet arrived, but your time is always at hand. ⁷ The world cannot hate you, but it does hate me because I testify about it — that its works are evil. ⁸ Go up to the festival yourselves. I'm not going up to this festival, because my time has not yet fully come." ⁹ After he had said these things, he stayed in Galilee

JESUS AT THE FESTIVAL OF SHELTERS

¹⁰ After his brothers had gone up to the festival, then he also went up, not openly but secretly. ¹¹ The Jews were looking for him at the festival and saying, "Where is he?" ¹² And there was a lot of murmuring about him among the crowds. Some were saying, "He's a good man." Others were saying, "No, on the contrary, he's deceiving the people." ¹³ Still, nobody was talking publicly about him for fear of the Jews.

¹⁴ When the festival was already half over, Jesus went up into the temple and began to teach. ¹⁵ Then the Jews were amazed and said, "How is this man so learned, since he hasn't been trained?"

¹⁶ Jesus answered them, "My teaching isn't mine but is from the one who sent me. ¹⁷ If anyone wants to do his will, he will know whether the teaching is from God or whether I am speaking on my own. ¹⁸ The one who speaks on his own seeks his own glory; but he who seeks the glory of the one who sent him is true, and there is no unrighteousness in him. ¹⁹ Didn't Moses give you the law? Yet none of you keeps the law. Why are you trying to kill me?"

²⁰ "You have a demon!" the crowd responded. "Who is trying to kill you?"

²¹ "I performed one work, and you are all amazed," Jesus answered. ²² "This is why Moses has given you circumcision — not that it comes from Moses but from the fathers — and you circumcise a man on the Sabbath. ²³ If a man receives circumcision on the Sabbath so that the law of Moses won't be broken, are you angry at me because I made a man entirely well on the Sabbath? ²⁴ Stop judging according to outward appearances; rather judge according to righteous judgment."

THE FEAST OF SHELTERS

Roughly six months after the conclusion of Passover in chapter 6, we find ourselves at the Festival of Shelters. This was one of three main feasts for Israelites (see Leviticus 23; Deuteronomy 6). At first Jesus said He wasn't going to go, but He later went secretly so as to not be seen as much in public since the Jews "were trying to kill him" (v. 1).

This feast took place in September or October, and thousands of Israelites traveled to Jerusalem and stayed in tents—a reminder of God's faithfulness while they were in the wilderness during the exodus. This was a festival of thanksgiving that proceeding the rainy season and anticipated the harvest the Lord would provide over the coming year. Little did the crowds know, God's greatest provision was walking among them.

In the crowds, Jesus overheard "murmuring" about who He was and took the opportunity to teach—to the amazement of all who heard. Jesus pointed away from Himself and to the Father, even saying that if their desire was to do God's will, they would be able to discern whether His teaching was from God (see v. 17).

But some in the crowd were still angry because Jesus had healed a disabled man on the Sabbath (see v. 21; see also John 5). Ironically their response to Jesus breaking the Sabbath was to kill Him on the Sabbath, which would also be against the law.

When we read these stories, we need to take note of the setting. Jesus is God's ultimate provision. Do we take the time to accept and receive Him? Will we see Him as the gift of grace that He is and allow His will to become our will as we follow Him and obey His teaching?

We do not celebrate the Festival of Shelters, but we can take time to celebrate God's provision to us in Jesus.

But to be believed, Jesus must be received.

REFLECTIONS

What does John 7:17 teach us about what it means to be disciples of Jesus?

If Jesus got His teaching "from the one who sent" Him (John 7:16), where do we get our teaching and understanding? How can we gain more understanding?

CONNECTING THE STORY

Jewish people celebrate God's provision, and ask for more of it, through the Festival of Tabernacles. Choose a time and a place this week to get alone with God. Thank Him for His goodness in your life, and ask Him for more of it!

JOHN 7:25-36

THE IDENTITY OF THE MESSIAH

[25] Some of the people of Jerusalem were saying, "Isn't this the man they are trying to kill? [26] Yet, look, he's speaking publicly and they're saying nothing to him. Can it be true that the authorities know he is the Messiah? [27] But we know where this man is from. When the Messiah comes, nobody will know where he is from."

[28] As he was teaching in the temple, Jesus cried out, "You know me and you know where I am from. Yet I have not come on my own, but the one who sent me is true. You don't know him; [29] I know him because I am from him, and he sent me."

[30] Then they tried to seize him. Yet no one laid a hand on him because his hour had not yet come. [31] However, many from the crowd believed in him and said, "When the Messiah comes, he won't perform more signs than this man has done, will he?" [32] The Pharisees heard the crowd murmuring these things about him, and so the chief priests and the Pharisees sent servants to arrest him.

[33] Then Jesus said, "I am only with you for a short time. Then I'm going to the one who sent me. [34] You will look for me, but you will not find me; and where I am, you cannot come."

[35] Then the Jews said to one another, "Where does he intend to go that we won't find him? He doesn't intend to go to the Jewish people dispersed among the Greeks and teach the Greeks, does he? [36] What is this remark he made: 'You will look for me, and you will not find me; and where I am, you cannot come'?"

YOU KNOW ME

One of the organizing features of John's Gospel is the idea of an elusive Messiah. Often Jesus intentionally went away from the crowds (see 7:6-9; 10:40-41; 11:56-57). Other times, Jesus avoided being taken or captured for supposed blasphemy (see 7:44; 8:59; 10:39). Jesus intentionally remained "hidden" until His hour—the time of His crucifixion—had come (see 12:23,27; 13:1; 16:32; 17:1).

Have you ever missed something hidden in plain sight? Many optical illusions work this way. We get so consumed looking at the minor details, we fail to notice the bigger picture. As the Festival of Shelters continued, Jesus continued to be misunderstood. Even as He directly shared His identity and motives, many consistently misunderstood and denied the truth. They missed what was right in front of them.

These denials were often related to minor quibbles about the law. This time, the denials centered around the fact that leaders knew where Jesus was from—Nazareth. This went against common Jewish teaching that the Messiah would be unknown until He came to announce salvation. But nestled in the middle of all of the misunderstanding, misinterpretation, and outright attempts to kill Jesus, we see a light. Hidden among the denials are affirmations of Jesus's true identity, two of which are here in verses 25 and 31.

These statements from the crowd are meant to lead us to John's intended conclusion—Jesus is the Messiah. Though hidden from many, Jesus is obvious to those are looking to Him with eyes of faith.

To see Jesus is to see God, and to find Jesus is to find life.

Even Jesus was misunderstood, but
He is seen by those who have faith to see.

REFLECTIONS

People misunderstood who Jesus was then as they do now. Who does our culture say Jesus is? How does that understanding square up with who Jesus claims to be?

In John people often failed to believe because they looked to the religious authorities instead of trusting the truth from Scripture. What are some things that stifle our belief?

Spend some time praying that you would have the eyes to see the work Jesus is doing in your life.

Old Testament
ALLUSIONS

Like most New Testament books, John draws many careful and planned parallels between the Old Testament. Learning to see these and becoming familiar with different parts of Scripture will not only help us understand John's Gospel better, it will also help us see Jesus better. There are multiple parallels between John 6 and Numbers 11. In this week's reading, we see that bread and manna are intricately connected.

Questions about resources

NUMBERS 11:13 | **JOHN 6:5**

Needing food where there is a lack of food

NUMBERS 11:22 | **JOHN 6:7–9**

The description of the manna

NUMBERS 11:7–9 | **JOHN 6:31**

People's grumbling

NUMBERS 11:1 | **JOHN 6:41,43**

Reference to the eating of meat/Jesus's "flesh"

NUMBERS 11:13 | **JOHN 6:51**[9]

JOHN 7:37-52

THE PROMISE OF THE SPIRIT

[37] On the last and most important day of the festival, Jesus stood up and cried out, "If anyone is thirsty, let him come to me and drink. [38] The one who believes in me, as the Scripture has said, will have streams of living water flow from deep within him." [39] He said this about the Spirit. Those who believed in Jesus were going to receive the Spirit, for the Spirit had not yet been given because Jesus had not yet been glorified.

THE PEOPLE ARE DIVIDED OVER JESUS

[40] When some from the crowd heard these words, they said, "This truly is the Prophet." [41] Others said, "This is the Messiah." But some said, "Surely the Messiah doesn't come from Galilee, does he? [42] Doesn't the Scripture say that the Messiah comes from David's offspring and from the town of Bethlehem, where David lived?" [43] So the crowd was divided because of him. [44] Some of them wanted to seize him, but no one laid hands on him.

DEBATE OVER JESUS'S CLAIMS

[45] Then the servants came to the chief priests and Pharisees, who asked them, "Why didn't you bring him?"

[46] The servants answered, "No man ever spoke like this!"

[47] Then the Pharisees responded to them, "Are you fooled too? [48] Have any of the rulers or Pharisees believed in him? [49] But this crowd, which doesn't know the law, is accursed."

[50] Nicodemus — the one who came to him previously and who was one of them — said to them, [51] "Our law doesn't judge a man before it hears from him and knows what he's doing, does it?"

[52] "You aren't from Galilee too, are you?" they replied. "Investigate and you will see that no prophet arises from Galilee."

<table>
<tr><td>DAY
26</td><td># TO ANYONE
WHO THIRSTS</td></tr>
</table>

TO ANYONE WHO THIRSTS

We've made it to the final day of the Festival of Shelters, and it's at this point that Jesus began to use His "outside voice." He'd stayed away from the celebrations until now, but not on this last day. Until now, Jesus had been relatively private with who He was and what He was on earth to do. But the whispering and quiet talk was over.

For eight straight days in this Festival of Shelters, all of the public teaching would center on water, with those in attendance praying and begging God to provide in the next season so their crops would grow and they'd have a harvest. The final day would conclude with two priests who would join together to pour out water and wine on the altar.

It was on this final day, in this moment, that Jesus decided to speak loudly and go fully public with His message and mission. Shouting so He could be heard over the chanting crowds, He said: "If anyone is thirsty, let him come to me and drink" (John 7:37). Do you catch the significance of this? At the end of several days of people crying out for water, Jesus acknowledged their physical desperation by standing up and saying that He was the water they needed. That He could quench their undying thirst. He brought the physical and spiritual together in a powerful way, fulfilling the core desires rooted in the Festival of Shelters.

With His words, He divided the crowd—it's a division that continues today. Though we seek fulfillment through countless avenues, Jesus came to fulfill the deepest longings of our hearts. All we have to do is receive the living water He offers.

Those who receive it have their thirst quenched in such a way that they will never be thirsty again.

Jesus provides streams of living
water for all who believe.

REFLECTIONS

Why is water such a helpful metaphor for this teaching?

Why do you think Jesus's words divided the crowd? Why did some believe while some wanted to seize Him?

CONNECTING THE STORY

John highlighted water throughout his Gospel for a variety of reasons. Whether it's Jesus turning water into wine (see John 2:1-11), explaining being born again to Nicodemus (see John 3:1-21), talking with the Samaritan woman at the well (see John 4), healing at the pool of Bethesda (see John 5:1-18), or this passage where Jesus is the water of life—water plays a significant role in John's Gospel. Though water was used physically, it has spiritual implications as well, most often centered around the Holy Spirit. Jesus's interactions with the woman at the well help us understand: The water Jesus offered would cause her to never thirst again (see John 4:13-14). Then in today's reading, John 7:38-39 makes it explicit: "'The one who believes in me, as the Scripture has said, will have streams of living water flow from deep within him.' He said this about the Spirit." The Spirit transforms, convicts, heals, and brings life. Now try rereading John's Gospel, and look for evidences of water that point to the Holy Spirit.

PAUSE & LISTEN
Spend some time reflecting over the week's reading.

Simon Peter answered, "Lord, to whom will we go? You have the words of eternal life. We have come to believe and know that you are the Holy One of God."

JOHN 6:68-69

DAY
28

REFLECTION

Use these questions for personal reflection or group discussion on John 6:22–7:52.

What stuck out to you most in this week's reading? What surprised you? Confused you?

What does this week's Scripture teach you about God and His character?

What does this week's Scripture teach you about humanity and our need for grace?

What five signs has John covered so far? Which resonates most with you?

In what way has your view of Jesus shifted since beginning this study?

PRAY

Throughout this week's reading, Jesus has called people to believe in Him. Pray this week and ask God to strengthen your belief. Despite the doubts, confusion, and challenges of life, ask that God would continue to lead you toward a deeper, more abiding belief in Jesus.

WEEK 5

I AM THE LIGHT OF THE WORLD

Receive the Light.

Nestled in the middle of this week's readings is one of the most controversial statements Jesus made during His earthly ministry. Though it may not seem like the most controversial to us, it incensed the Jewish leaders so much they picked up rocks to stone Him.

In John 8:58, Jesus told them, "before Abraham was, I am." Saying this, Jesus had invoked the personal name of the One true God and equated Himself with God the Father. The Jewish leaders thought this was blasphemous and responded accordingly.

Much of the Scripture this week deals with themes of light and darkness. Not only is Jesus the Light of the world who brings light to the blind—physically and spiritually—He is also the One who called light out of darkness.

He is the Light of the world, and He is calling us to receive Him.

JOHN 8:1-20

8 [53 Then each one went to his house. 1 But Jesus went to the Mount of Olives.

AN ADULTERESS FORGIVEN

2 At dawn he went to the temple again, and all the people were coming to him. He sat down and began to teach them.

3 Then the scribes and the Pharisees brought a woman caught in adultery, making her stand in the center. 4 "Teacher," they said to him, "this woman was caught in the act of committing adultery. 5 In the law Moses commanded us to stone such women. So what do you say?" 6 They asked this to trap him, in order that they might have evidence to accuse him.

Jesus stooped down and started writing on the ground with his finger. 7 When they persisted in questioning him, he stood up and said to them, "The one without sin among you should be the first to throw a stone at her." 8 Then he stooped down again and continued writing on the ground. 9 When they heard this, they left one by one, starting with the older men. Only he was left, with the woman in the center. 10 When Jesus stood up, he said to her, "Woman, where are they? Has no one condemned you?"

11 "No one, Lord," she answered.

"Neither do I condemn you," said Jesus. "Go, and from now on do not sin anymore."]

THE LIGHT OF THE WORLD

12 Jesus spoke to them again: "I am the light of the world. Anyone who follows me will never walk in the darkness but will have the light of life."

13 So the Pharisees said to him, "You are testifying about yourself. Your testimony is not valid."

14 "Even if I testify about myself," Jesus replied, "My testimony is true, because I know where I came from and where I'm going. But you don't know where I come from or where I'm going. 15 You judge by human standards. I judge no one. 16 And if I do judge, my judgment is true, because it is not I alone who judge, but I and the Father who sent me. 17 Even in your law it is written that the testimony of two witnesses is true. 18 I am the one who testifies about myself, and the Father who sent me testifies about me."

19 Then they asked him, "Where is your Father?"

"You know neither me nor my Father," Jesus answered. "If you knew me, you would also know my Father." 20 He spoke these words by the treasury, while teaching in the temple. But no one seized him, because his hour had not yet come.

[The earliest manuscripts omit 7:53–8:11.]

LIGHT AND DARK

Have you ever lost power to your home and had to feel around in the darkness for a flashlight or some matches to light a candle? Or have you ever had to use your phone to navigate a dark and unfamiliar space?

Something you learn in these situations is that light always responds to darkness. No matter how deep the darkness or how faint the light—light always pierces darkness. Though the effects may be small, they are noticeable. John frequently employs metaphors of light and darkness to describe Jesus. He learned to use these metaphors by listening to Jesus teach.

Jesus is "the light of the world" (v. 12) who promises His followers a light of life that will always break through the darkness. Jesus said this about Himself, and His testimony was verified by God the Father through the miraculous signs Jesus performed throughout this book.

Each miracle, each sign is a bright light shining into a dark world. It's a breaking-in of the kingdom of God—and it is an announcement that Jesus is the light and the path of His light will lead us out of darkness.

That's what He was showing when He found a woman who had been used and discarded by men as well as these scribes and Pharisees who exploited her sin and disregarded her humanity to make a point.

Jesus looked at her, saw her, saw the sin of her accusers, pierced the darkness, and forged a path to forgiveness and redemption with His light.

The path remains for us to follow, whatever darkness we encounter.

Jesus is the Light of the world.

REFLECTIONS

What does it mean for Jesus to be the Light of the world?

How has Jesus been a light in darkness to you?

How would you feel if you were caught in your sin and then paraded in front of the church as a pawn? What emotions would be running through your mind and heart? How would those emotions shift when Jesus didn't condemn you but set you free?

JESUS PREDICTS HIS DEPARTURE

[21] Then he said to them again, "I'm going away; you will look for me, and you will die in your sin. Where I'm going, you cannot come."

[22] So the Jews said again, "He won't kill himself, will he, since he says, 'Where I'm going, you cannot come'?"

[23] "You are from below," he told them, "I am from above. You are of this world; I am not of this world. [24] Therefore I told you that you will die in your sins. For if you do not believe that I am he, you will die in your sins."

[25] "Who are you?" they questioned.

"Exactly what I've been telling you from the very beginning," Jesus told them. [26] "I have many things to say and to judge about you, but the one who sent me is true, and what I have heard from him — these things I tell the world."

[27] They did not know he was speaking to them about the Father. [28] So Jesus said to them, "When you lift up the Son of Man, then you will know that I am he, and that I do nothing on my own. But just as the Father taught me, I say these things. [29] The one who sent me is with me. He has not left me alone, because I always do what pleases him."

TRUTH AND FREEDOM

[30] As he was saying these things, many believed in him.

[31] Then Jesus said to the Jews who had believed him, "If you continue in my word, you really are my disciples. [32] You will know the truth, and the truth will set you free."

[33] "We are descendants of Abraham," they answered him, "and we have never been enslaved to anyone. How can you say, 'You will become free'?"

[34] Jesus responded, "Truly I tell you, everyone who commits sin is a slave of sin. [35] A slave does not remain in the household forever, but a son does remain forever. [36] So if the Son sets you free, you really will be free. [37] I know you are descendants of Abraham, but you are trying to kill me because my word has no place among you. [38] I speak what I have seen in the presence of the Father; so then, you do what you have heard from your father."

[39] "Our father is Abraham," they replied.

"If you were Abraham's children," Jesus told them, "you would do what Abraham did. [40] But now you are trying to kill me, a man who has told you the truth that I heard from God. Abraham did not do this. [41] You're doing what your father does."

"We weren't born of sexual immorality," they said. "We have one Father — God."

[42] Jesus said to them, "If God were your Father, you would love me, because I came from God and I am here. For I didn't come on my own, but he sent me. [43] Why don't you understand what I say? Because you cannot listen to my word. [44] You are of your father the devil, and you want to carry out your father's desires. He was a murderer from the beginning and does not stand in the truth, because there is no truth in him. When he tells a lie, he speaks from his own nature, because he is a liar and the father of lies. [45] Yet because I tell the truth, you do not believe me. [46] Who among you can convict me of sin? If I am telling the truth, why don't you believe me? [47] The one who is from God listens to God's words. This is why you don't listen, because you are not from God."

JESUS AND ABRAHAM

[48] The Jews responded to him, "Aren't we right in saying that you're a Samaritan and have a demon?"

[49] "I do not have a demon," Jesus answered. "On the contrary, I honor my Father and you dishonor me. [50] I do not seek my own glory; there is one who seeks it and judges. [51] Truly I tell you, if anyone keeps my word, he will never see death."

[52] Then the Jews said, "Now we know you have a demon. Abraham died and so did the prophets. You say, 'If anyone keeps my word, he will never taste death.' [53] Are you greater than our father Abraham who died? And the prophets died. Who do you claim to be?"

[54] "If I glorify myself," Jesus answered, "my glory is nothing. My Father — about whom you say, 'He is our God' — he is the one who glorifies me. [55] You do not know him, but I know him. If I were to say I don't know him, I would be a liar like you. But I do know him, and I keep his word. [56] Your father Abraham rejoiced to see my day; he saw it and was glad."

[57] The Jews replied, "You aren't fifty years old yet, and you've seen Abraham?"

[58] Jesus said to them, "Truly I tell you, before Abraham was, I am."

[59] So they picked up stones to throw at him. But Jesus was hidden and went out of the temple.

<table>
<tr><td>DAY
30</td><td></td></tr>
</table>

THE I AM

At times when we read Jesus's words, particularly if they are new to us, we might find what He says cryptic or confusing. Time and culture has separated us from Jesus's earthly ministry, but one clue about how to interpret Jesus's words is to look at the way people responded.

The Pharisees understood clearly what Jesus was saying—He was claiming to be God. He was declaring that He's the Son of God who existed before the Jewish patriarch Abraham and who has the ability to pardon sin and grant eternal life.

All He said was: "I am." In those two words, Jesus gave Himself the great name of God, the name that defines an eternal existence—One who has always been and will always be. Jews wouldn't even speak this name, and Jesus not only publicly spoke it, but He also claimed it as His name.

Though the Pharisees had witnessed the miracles and signs of Jesus, they didn't believe in the One who was performing them. It's one thing to witness a miracle; it's quite another to choose to act based on what you've seen. They were locked in their ways of thinking; they were slaves to their sinful thoughts and actions.

Yet Jesus, in His kindness, offered freedom. Freedom from having to be born in a certain family, look a certain way, or having to live a perfect life. In short: Jesus died to free us from our sin and all of its implications.

The Pharisees would deny it, but they, like us, were in the presence of the Creator. But for them and for us—if the Son sets you free, you are free indeed.

Those the Son has set free are free indeed.

REFLECTIONS

In John 8:25-30, the Pharisees hurled four distinct challenges at Jesus's claims. What were they? How do these questions show the foolishness of the Pharisees?

What does it mean for Jesus to set you free? How has Jesus freed you?

CONNECTING THE STORY

God revealed His name to Moses in Exodus 3—"I am" (Exodus 3:14). God's name is so sacred in many Jewish circles that it cannot be publicly spoken even to this day, with preference given to Adonai in prayer and Hashem in conversations. "I am that I am" is the English translation, but the Hebrew word is just consonants, no vowels: YHWH. It denotes the eternal existence, self-existence, and completeness of God. And when Jesus refers to Himself with the same name, He acknowledges that He and God the Father are one and the same.

I am.

One of the features of John's Gospel is the seven "I am" statements Jesus made. Each of these reveals something about Jesus's nature and character. When He made these statements, He was intentionally evoking the personal name of God to state His equality and unity with God the Father.

"I am the bread of life."

JOHN 6:35. Jesus is the One who satisfies spiritual hunger.

"I am the light of the world."

JOHN 8:12. Jesus overwhelms and overcomes sin and darkness.

"I am the gate for the sheep."

JOHN 10:7. Jesus protects His followers from those who would harm them.

"I am the good shepherd."

JOHN 10:11. Jesus cares for and watches over His followers.

"I am the resurrection and the life."

JOHN 11:25. Jesus brings and gives eternal life.

"I am the way, the truth, and the life."

JOHN 14:6. Jesus is the source of knowledge about God.

"I am the true vine."

JOHN 15:1. Jesus connects His followers to spiritual vitality.

JOHN 9:1-12

THE SIXTH SIGN: HEALING A MAN BORN BLIND

9 As he was passing by, he saw a man blind from birth. [2] His disciples asked him, "Rabbi, who sinned, this man or his parents, that he was born blind?"

[3] "Neither this man nor his parents sinned," Jesus answered. "This came about so that God's works might be displayed in him. [4] We must do the works of him who sent me while it is day. Night is coming when no one can work. [5] As long as I am in the world, I am the light of the world."

[6] After he said these things he spit on the ground, made some mud from the saliva, and spread the mud on his eyes. [7] "Go," he told him, "wash in the pool of Siloam" (which means "Sent"). So he left, washed, and came back seeing.

[8] His neighbors and those who had seen him before as a beggar said, "Isn't this the one who used to sit begging?" [9] Some said, "He's the one." Others were saying, "No, but he looks like him."

He kept saying, "I'm the one."

[10] So they asked him, "Then how were your eyes opened?"

[11] He answered, "The man called Jesus made mud, spread it on my eyes, and told me, 'Go to Siloam and wash.' So when I went and washed I received my sight."

[12] "Where is he?" they asked.

"I don't know," he said.

HEALING THE BLIND

In John 8, Jesus disclosed that He is the light of the world (see v. 12). In John 9, Jesus provided literal and spiritual light to man who had been born blind. As the disciples approached this blind man they could only imagine two reasons why he could have been born blind—either he sinned or his parents did. This was a common Jewish assumption in the first century.

While it's true that certain sin can lead to suffering, that's not what was going on here. Jesus offered an alternative: neither this man's sin nor his parents' resulted in blindness. The reason Jesus provided was one they never imagined—this man was blind so that God's power could be shown in him.

As often is the case, those around Jesus were too focused on lesser issues to appreciate what Jesus was about to do. The disciples wanted to use this moment to clarify a theological truth (about which they were wrong), and Jesus wanted to heal a blind man and display the power of God.

Notice that the man didn't ask to be healed, but Jesus—seeing His disciples talk *about* a man instead of *to* him—bent down, made mud, spread it on the man's eyes, and told him to wash. Then the man was healed. Jesus engaged the man, touched him, talked to him, and healed him.

The Old Testament predicted that the coming Messiah would cure blindness (see Isaiah 29:18; 35:5; 42:7). And with this sign, the sixth in John's Gospel, we see Him doing just that: fulfilling an Old Testament prophecy and further proving His identity as the Messiah.

He is the Light of the world who has come to free us from physical and spiritual blindness.

Jesus redeems physical and spiritual blindness.

REFLECTIONS

How else in John's Gospel have you seen Jesus take time to speak to and humanize someone who was disregarded?

What does Jesus's interaction with this man teach us about His heart for sinners and sufferers?

What does it look like to love and serve others like Jesus?

THE HEALED MAN'S TESTIMONY

[13] They brought the man who used to be blind to the Pharisees. [14] The day that Jesus made the mud and opened his eyes was a Sabbath. [15] Then the Pharisees asked him again how he received his sight.

"He put mud on my eyes," he told them. "I washed and I can see."

[16] Some of the Pharisees said, "This man is not from God, because he doesn't keep the Sabbath." But others were saying, "How can a sinful man perform such signs?" And there was a division among them.

[17] Again they asked the blind man, "What do you say about him, since he opened your eyes?"

"He's a prophet," he said.

[18] The Jews did not believe this about him — that he was blind and received sight — until they summoned the parents of the one who had received his sight.

[19] They asked them, "Is this your son, the one you say was born blind? How then does he now see?"

[20] "We know this is our son and that he was born blind," his parents answered. [21] "But we don't know how he now sees, and we don't know who opened his eyes. Ask him; he's of age. He will speak for himself." [22] His parents said these things because they were afraid of the Jews, since the Jews had already agreed that if anyone confessed him as the Messiah, he would be banned from the synagogue. [23] This is why his parents said, "He's of age; ask him."

[24] So a second time they summoned the man who had been blind and told him, "Give glory to God. We know that this man is a sinner."

[25] He answered, "Whether or not he's a sinner, I don't know. One thing I do know: I was blind, and now I can see!"

[26] Then they asked him, "What did he do to you? How did he open your eyes?"

[27] "I already told you," he said, "and you didn't listen. Why do you want to hear it again? You don't want to become his disciples too, do you?"

[28] They ridiculed him: "You're that man's disciple, but we're Moses's disciples. [29] We know that God has spoken to Moses. But this man — we don't know where he's from."

[30] "This is an amazing thing!" the man told them. "You don't know where he is from, and yet he opened my eyes. [31] We know that God doesn't listen to sinners, but if anyone is God-fearing and does his will, he listens to him. [32] Throughout history no one has ever heard of someone opening the eyes of a person born blind. [33] If this man were not from God, he wouldn't be able to do anything."

[34] "You were born entirely in sin," they replied, "and are you trying to teach us?" Then they threw him out.

SPIRITUAL BLINDNESS

[35] Jesus heard that they had thrown the man out, and when he found him, he asked, "Do you believe in the Son of Man?"

[36] "Who is he, Sir, that I may believe in him?" he asked.

[37] Jesus answered, "You have seen him; in fact, he is the one speaking with you."

[38] "I believe, Lord!" he said, and he worshiped him.

[39] Jesus said, "I came into this world for judgment, in order that those who do not see will see and those who do see will become blind."

[40] Some of the Pharisees who were with him heard these things and asked him, "We aren't blind too, are we?"

[41] "If you were blind," Jesus told them, "you wouldn't have sin. But now that you say, 'We see,' your sin remains.

SIGHT RESTORED

It's possible to be so devoted to keeping the rules that we end up neglecting our devotion to God. It's possible to be so concerned with keeping every minor point of the law that we miss the major point. Jesus chided the Pharisees for doing just that, keeping the tiny laws but neglecting "justice, mercy, and faithfulness" (Matthew 23:23).

In these verses John takes us away from Jesus and His encounter with the blind man to allow us to eavesdrop on a conversation the Pharisees were having about the blind man. They were mad again because Jesus healed a man on the Sabbath. Not only did Jesus heal, but He also performed work that was outlawed in Jewish tradition. Making clay or pottery was one of thirty-nine types of work forbidden on the Sabbath.

Then, they encountered a man who claimed to have his blindness healed. This man's parents were so afraid of the powerful Pharisees—who used their power to keep anyone who acknowledged Jesus as the Messiah from the temple—that they wouldn't defend their son. The man had to defend himself. The Pharisees heard the man's story, dismissed him, then invited him back a second time to recount his story. Instead of cowering, the man continued boldly, even becoming an evangelist to his accusers: "I was blind, and now I can see!" (John 9:25).

And the Pharisees did throw the man out of the temple. After this, Jesus approached the man and asked him a question that remains relevant to us today: "Do you believe in the Son of Man?" (John 9:35).

Every person who has ever lived must answer that question. Jesus went on to unpack that His removing physical blindness is reflective of Him also removing spiritual blindness. And we are all victims of spiritual blindness. Jesus proves His divinity by curing both.

Jesus gives the spiritual sight to see as He does.

REFLECTIONS

What does it teach us about Jesus that He sought out the formerly blind man after the Pharisees harassed him?

How do you answer Jesus's question in John 9:35? How does your life reflect your answer?

Do you have a story of Jesus giving you (spiritual) sight? Who can you share that with this week?

JOHN 10:1-21

THE GOOD SHEPHERD

10 "Truly I tell you, anyone who doesn't enter the sheep pen by the gate but climbs in some other way is a thief and a robber. [2] The one who enters by the gate is the shepherd of the sheep. [3] The gatekeeper opens it for him, and the sheep hear his voice. He calls his own sheep by name and leads them out. [4] When he has brought all his own outside, he goes ahead of them. The sheep follow him because they know his voice. [5] They will never follow a stranger; instead they will run away from him, because they don't know the voice of strangers." [6] Jesus gave them this figure of speech, but they did not understand what he was telling them.

[7] Jesus said again, "Truly I tell you, I am the gate for the sheep. [8] All who came before me are thieves and robbers, but the sheep didn't listen to them. [9] I am the gate. If anyone enters by me, he will be saved and will come in and go out and find pasture. [10] A thief comes only to steal and kill and destroy. I have come so that they may have life and have it in abundance.

[11] "I am the good shepherd. The good shepherd lays down his life for the sheep. [12] The hired hand, since he is not the shepherd and doesn't own the sheep, leaves them and runs away when he sees a wolf coming. The wolf then snatches and scatters them. [13] This happens because he is a hired hand and doesn't care about the sheep.

[14] "I am the good shepherd. I know my own, and my own know me, [15] just as the Father knows me, and I know the Father. I lay down my life for the sheep. [16] But I have other sheep that are not from this sheep pen; I must bring them also, and they will listen to my voice. Then there will be one flock, one shepherd. [17] This is why the Father loves me, because I lay down my life so that I may take it up again. [18] No one takes it from me, but I lay it down on my own. I have the right to lay it down, and I have the right to take it up again. I have received this command from my Father."

[19] Again the Jews were divided because of these words. [20] Many of them were saying, "He has a demon and he's crazy. Why do you listen to him?" [21] Others were saying, "These aren't the words of someone who is demon-possessed. Can a demon open the eyes of the blind?"

<table>
<tr><td>DAY
33</td><td></td></tr>
</table>

NOT JUST A SHEPHERD— THE SHEPHERD

If you'll remember Jesus's first sign in chapter 2, He mentioned that His time had not come (see v. 4). As we work through John's Gospel, Jesus steadily reveals more about Himself. We get a better understanding of who He is and what He came to do as we continue reading. This passage is no exception.

Using images His audience would've easily understood, Jesus revealed that He is the Good Shepherd. While you might not have a frame of reference for shepherds and their work, everyone listening to Jesus that day did. Sheep are entirely dependent on their shepherd for their constant protection and care. They are defenseless and need to be led to have even their most basic needs met.

To be the gate of the sheep is to be the entry point and protection. The shepherd stands in the door to push away all who would harm them. That is what Jesus offers to all the sheep of His pasture. He is the Good Shepherd. He sacrifices Himself for His sheep. Jesus welcomes people of every tribe, tongue, and nation to enter His sheep pen, where they find rest and protection (see v. 16; Revelation 7:9).

Following Jesus tunes our ears and our hearts to recognize His voice and respond to it, like sheep would for their shepherd. We build a relationship and trust over time as we experience His care. Our lives are more important to our Shepherd than His own.

Jesus reveals here that it is His plan to lay down His life for His sheep; to sacrifice Himself so that all who trust in Him would flourish. The Jews listening to Him found this teaching difficult and tough to believe. It led them to doubt the work He did for the blind man. But those who find pasture with this Shepherd find the light and life John promised at the beginning of his Gospel (see 1:4).

Jesus is the Good Shepherd who sacrifices His life for His sheep.

REFLECTIONS

List all of the things Jesus claims He will do for His sheep in this passage.

How do we learn to hear Jesus's voice and respond to Him as sheep would to their shepherd?

CONNECTING THE STORY

The motif of shepherd is found throughout the Old Testament. Jacob referred to God as his Shepherd (see Genesis 48:15); Moses, David, and the patriarchs were all shepherds; and as a Middle Eastern, agrarian society, the Israelites were familiar with shepherding. And we, as the people of God, are prone to act like sheep. Isaiah 53:6a reminds us, "We all went astray like sheep; we all have turned to our own way." Then Isaiah points us to Someone coming who would receive the punishment we deserve: "And the LORD has punished him for the iniquity of us all" (Isaiah 53:6b). We're all sheep in need of a Shepherd, and while previous shepherds were helpful, they failed us. We need a Good Shepherd, One who is perfect in every way and would lay down His life for us, His sheep.

PAUSE & LISTEN

Spend some time reflecting over the week's reading.

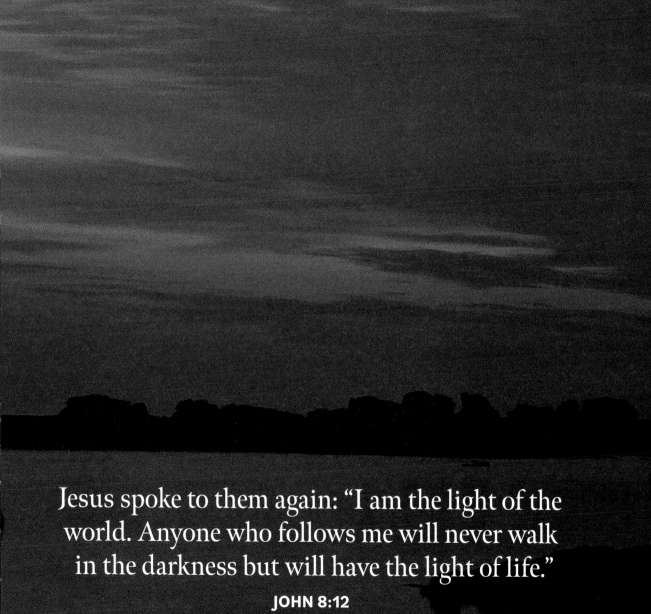

Jesus spoke to them again: "I am the light of the world. Anyone who follows me will never walk in the darkness but will have the light of life."

JOHN 8:12

REFLECTION

Use these questions for personal reflection or group discussion on John 8:1–10:21.

What stuck out to you most in this week's reading? What surprised you? Confused you?

What does this week's Scripture teach you about God and His character?

What does this week's Scripture teach you about humanity and our need for grace?

How does this week's Scripture point you to Jesus?

This week, we saw Jesus breaking some cultural, "religious" rules. If Jesus were physically present today, what religious rules do you think He might break?

PRAY

Petition God, the Light of the universe, who gives us light to dispel the darkness, that He would give you insight. Because "those who have insight will shine like the bright expanse of the heavens, and those who lead many to righteousness, like the stars forever and ever" (Daniel 12:3).

I AM THE RESURRECTION AND THE LIFE

With Jesus, resurrection
has the final word.

This week includes the last and most powerful sign proving Jesus is the Son of God, the resurrection of Lazarus. This whole week is situated in John chapter 11. As we read, take notice of the Man you've been reading about throughout our time in John.

See how deliberate He is in word and deed.

See how sensitive He is to the needs of His friends.

See His very real grief over the death of a close friend.

See the calm power He possesses bring His dead friend back to life.

Believe Jesus is resurrection and life.

JOHN 10:22-42

JESUS AT THE FESTIVAL OF DEDICATION

²² Then the Festival of Dedication took place in Jerusalem, and it was winter. ²³ Jesus was walking in the temple in Solomon's Colonnade. ²⁴ The Jews surrounded him and asked, "How long are you going to keep us in suspense? If you are the Messiah, tell us plainly."

²⁵ "I did tell you and you don't believe," Jesus answered them. "The works that I do in my Father's name testify about me. ²⁶ But you don't believe because you are not of my sheep. ²⁷ My sheep hear my voice, I know them, and they follow me. ²⁸ I give them eternal life, and they will never perish. No one will snatch them out of my hand. ²⁹ My Father, who has given them to me, is greater than all. No one is able to snatch them out of the Father's hand. ³⁰ I and the Father are one."

RENEWED EFFORTS TO STONE JESUS

³¹ Again the Jews picked up rocks to stone him.

³² Jesus replied, "I have shown you many good works from the Father. For which of these works are you stoning me?"

³³ "We aren't stoning you for a good work," the Jews answered, "but for blasphemy, because you — being a man — make yourself God."

³⁴ Jesus answered them, "Isn't it written in your law, **I said, you are gods**? ³⁵ If he called those to whom the word of God came 'gods' — and the Scripture cannot be broken — ³⁶ do you say, 'You are blaspheming' to the one the Father set apart and sent into the world, because I said: I am the Son of God? ³⁷ If I am not doing my Father's works, don't believe me. ³⁸ But if I am doing them and you don't believe me, believe the works. This way you will know and understand that the Father is in me and I in the Father." ³⁹ Then they were trying again to seize him, but he escaped their grasp.

MANY BEYOND THE JORDAN BELIEVE IN JESUS

⁴⁰ So he departed again across the Jordan to the place where John had been baptizing earlier, and he remained there. ⁴¹ Many came to him and said, "John never did a sign, but everything John said about this man was true." ⁴² And many believed in him there.

HIS WORD AND HIS WORK

The Festival of Dedication, also called the Feast of Lights, is celebrated today as Hanukkah, and that's where we find Jesus in this passage. These details help us mark time throughout John's Gospel.

Here, Jesus was walking in the temple in Solomon's colonnades, surrounded by Jews who just wanted Jesus to tell them if He was the Messiah or not. This was not a genuine question; their actions revealed who they clearly believed He was. Jesus had already shown in word and deed that He was the Jewish Messiah; their refusal to accept Jesus at His word was clear. Hopefully you've noticed this kind of interaction throughout the book of John, where Jesus was placed "on trial" by crowds and onlookers who demanded that He prove Himself.

John supports Jesus's claims at trial by presenting many witnesses to Jesus's identity. From His own mouth and from His own hands, we see Jesus is God. Jesus argued this point in these verses (see vv. 31-39). The evidence is overwhelming, and John organized his Gospel this way so that we may believe (see 20:31).

His works and His words speak louder than any doubt of suspicion. Those who believe belong to Jesus, and no one can ever snatch them from His hands (see v. 28). In Him, we find rest and security that cannot be found anywhere else.

Once again, the leaders willfully denied Jesus's claim and sought to stone Him. For those determined not to believe, no proof is enough. But here John is asking you to see Jesus's works and hear His words and believe again today.

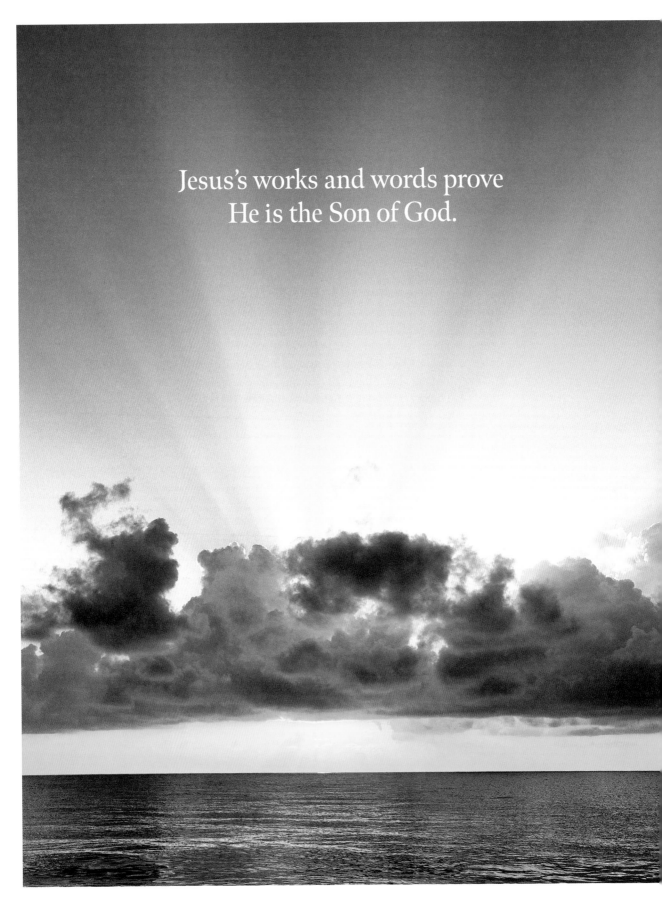

Jesus's works and words prove
He is the Son of God.

REFLECTIONS

How would you explain John 10:28-30 in your own words?

What part of your belief about Jesus needs to change this week to more fully align with Scripture?

What about your work and your words show that you are a disciple of Jesus?

JOHN 11:1-27

LAZARUS DIES AT BETHANY

11 Now a man was sick, Lazarus from Bethany, the village of Mary and her sister Martha. [2] Mary was the one who anointed the Lord with perfume and wiped his feet with her hair, and it was her brother Lazarus who was sick. [3] So the sisters sent a message to him: "Lord, the one you love is sick."

[4] When Jesus heard it, he said, "This sickness will not end in death but is for the glory of God, so that the Son of God may be glorified through it." [5] Now Jesus loved Martha, her sister, and Lazarus. [6] So when he heard that he was sick, he stayed two more days in the place where he was. [7] Then after that, he said to the disciples, "Let's go to Judea again."

[8] "Rabbi," the disciples told him, "just now the Jews tried to stone you, and you're going there again?"

[9] "Aren't there twelve hours in a day?" Jesus answered. "If anyone walks during the day, he doesn't stumble, because he sees the light of this world. [10] But if anyone walks during the night, he does stumble, because the light is not in him."

[11] He said this, and then he told them, "Our friend Lazarus has fallen asleep, but I'm on my way to wake him up."

[12] Then the disciples said to him, "Lord, if he has fallen asleep, he will get well."

[13] Jesus, however, was speaking about his death, but they thought he was speaking about natural sleep. [14] So Jesus then told them plainly, "Lazarus has died. [15] I'm glad for you that I wasn't there so that you may believe. But let's go to him."

[16] Then Thomas (called "Twin") said to his fellow disciples, "Let's go too so that we may die with him."

THE RESURRECTION AND THE LIFE

[17] When Jesus arrived, he found that Lazarus had already been in the tomb four days. [18] Bethany was near Jerusalem (less than two miles away). [19] Many of the Jews had come to Martha and Mary to comfort them about their brother.

[20] As soon as Martha heard that Jesus was coming, she went to meet him, but Mary remained seated in the house. [21] Then Martha said to Jesus, "Lord, if you had been here, my brother wouldn't have died. [22] Yet even now I know that whatever you ask from God, God will give you."

[23] "Your brother will rise again," Jesus told her.

[24] Martha said to him, "I know that he will rise again in the resurrection at the last day."

[25] Jesus said to her, "I am the resurrection and the life. The one who believes in me, even if he dies, will live. [26] Everyone who lives and believes in me will never die. Do you believe this?"

[27] "Yes, Lord," she told him, "I believe you are the Messiah, the Son of God, who comes into the world."

RESURRECTION AND LIFE

John is the only Gospel writer that includes the story of the death and resurrection of Lazarus. His reason lies in the purpose for which he wrote his Gospel: to prove that Jesus was the Son of God. The remaining days in this week will be devoted to looking closely at the seventh sign.

This seventh sign provides irrefutable proof that Jesus has power over life and death because He is the resurrection and the life.

The story has an odd beginning: Jesus heard that His good friend, Lazarus, was sick and intentionally decided to wait two additional days before going to him. In those days Lazarus died, which further confused Jesus's disciples. But He did this "so that you may believe" (v. 15). Jesus wanted them (and us) to understand this wasn't a "healing" story; it's a resurrection story.

By the time Jesus arrived, Lazarus had been dead for four days. This gave Jesus a chance to further explain both the meaning for this upcoming sign and His purpose for being on earth. He doesn't just have power over parts of life—Jesus is life itself. He stated this plainly and asked Lazarus's sister, Martha, a question for all of us to answer:

> "The one who believes in me, even if he dies, will live. Everyone who lives and believes in me will never die. *Do you believe this?*"
> **—JOHN 11:25**

John asks us to examine the evidence and believe. But maybe while examining the evidence, you've gotten lost in the weeds. Maybe you need to step back and answer Jesus's question—"Do you believe this?"

Do you believe Jesus is resurrection and life? Do you believe the key to abundant life belongs to Him? Will you press in and see Jesus for who He is and accept what He offers? It is yours through faith.

He is the resurrection and the life.

REFLECTIONS

Why did Jesus wait to visit with His sick and dying friend, Lazarus (see vv. 13-15)?

How does this passage shape your beliefs about sickness, pain, and even death?

Why is it important that we take the time to answer the questions Jesus asked for ourselves?

JOHN 11:28-37

JESUS SHARES THE SORROW OF DEATH

²⁸ Having said this, she went back and called her sister Mary, saying in private, "The Teacher is here and is calling for you."

²⁹ As soon as Mary heard this, she got up quickly and went to him. ³⁰ Jesus had not yet come into the village but was still in the place where Martha had met him. ³¹ The Jews who were with her in the house consoling her saw that Mary got up quickly and went out. They followed her, supposing that she was going to the tomb to cry there.

³² As soon as Mary came to where Jesus was and saw him, she fell at his feet and told him, "Lord, if you had been here, my brother wouldn't have died!"

³³ When Jesus saw her crying, and the Jews who had come with her crying, he was deeply moved in his spirit and troubled. ³⁴ "Where have you put him?" he asked.

"Lord," they told him, "come and see."

³⁵ Jesus wept.

³⁶ So the Jews said, "See how he loved him!" ³⁷ But some of them said, "Couldn't he who opened the blind man's eyes also have kept this man from dying?"

DAY 38

JESUS WEPT

Have you ever questioned God about something? That's what Martha did in yesterday's reading. Her beloved brother had died, and she was looking for answers. Today, we see Mary's reaction to the same event. Instead of answers, she wanted comfort.

Have you ever been there? Maybe you experienced something that you just couldn't explain, that didn't make sense, or that just seemed to cause pointless pain. And it caused you to cry out to the God of the universe, longing for answers or comfort.

That's the sense we get in Mary's desperate cry as she wept over her brother's death. Her words and emotions were so heavy that they even moved Jesus. Pain has a way of drawing out some of our deepest emotions.

Yet in her desperation, Mary declared something important: she acknowledged that Jesus could have prevented this death because He alone has the power to prevent it. Yet for all His power and authority—Jesus joined Mary and wept at the death of His friend. Overcome by emotion and grief, Jesus cried.

These weren't tears of hopelessness and helplessness, though. Jesus has the power to fix anything. In fact, we're going to read His response tomorrow. Jesus was displaying meekness—harnessed power—here. Still, the Jewish mourners saw how much Jesus loved Lazarus. Jesus enters into our pain because of His love for us.

Jesus is sovereign—in total control of all life's circumstances, including death. He's also close to us—ready to meet is in our need, whatever that need may be. Martha wanted answers; Mary wanted comfort. Jesus provided both.

He wept over the death of His friend.

REFLECTIONS

Compare and contrast what Martha and Mary said to and wanted from Jesus over the last two days of reading.

Think of the deepest pain you've ever experienced. How does it make you feel to realize that Jesus has entered your pain and relates to you in that moment?

Who might you need to support and comfort in their grief and pain? Why is this a privilege for followers of Jesus?

JOHN 11: 38-44

THE SEVENTH SIGN: RAISING LAZARUS FROM THE DEAD

[38] Then Jesus, deeply moved again, came to the tomb. It was a cave, and a stone was lying against it. [39] "Remove the stone," Jesus said.

Martha, the dead man's sister, told him, "Lord, there is already a stench because he has been dead four days."

[40] Jesus said to her, "Didn't I tell you that if you believed you would see the glory of God?"

[41] So they removed the stone. Then Jesus raised his eyes and said, "Father, I thank you that you heard me. [42] I know that you always hear me, but because of the crowd standing here I said this, so that they may believe you sent me." [43] After he said this, he shouted with a loud voice, "Lazarus, come out!" [44] The dead man came out bound hand and foot with linen strips and with his face wrapped in a cloth. Jesus said to them, "Unwrap him and let him go."

THE SEVENTH SIGN

At this point, Lazarus had been dead for four days. This was significant because the *Talmud* (a compilation of ancient Jewish teachings) says that "for three days long the soul returns to the grave, thinking that it will return (into the body); when however it sees that the color of its face has changed then it goes away and leaves it. Four days in the grave establishes that all was over."[10] Simply put, Jewish teaching would've declared Lazarus dead. On top of that, additional evidence abounded: Lazarus was in a tomb with a stone rolled in front, and Mary was picking up a foul odor.

Then Jesus called Lazarus by name to come out of the tomb, presumably because if He just generically said, "Come out," all of the dead would've risen: Jesus has the power over all life and death.

Lazarus stumbled out of the tomb in front of the entire gathered crowd, still wrapped in his burial cloths but very much alive.

So what was the point of this sign? Jesus Himself tells us: "So that they may believe [God] sent me" (John 11:42). Jesus didn't haphazardly perform a miracle for a friend He loved. He had a deeper purpose: to help others believe Jesus was who He claimed to be. Dead people don't resurrect themselves; they're dead. This sign undeniably declared that Jesus is God, and He holds the power over life and death.

Through this, Jesus's divinity was put on display. Everyone watching would've known that only God had the power over death like this. This final sign sealed all of Jesus's claims and rests John's case that Jesus is who He said He was and would accomplish what He came to accomplish.

Jesus has the power to call
the dead back to life.

REFLECTIONS

According to this passage, would there have been any doubt that Lazarus was truly dead? Why was this significant?

As you've read through the seven signs in John's Gospel, is there one that has affected you more than the others? If so, why?

This week, pray for an opportunity to share about the perfect timing of God as it relates to this passage and your life.

Repeated Language *in* John

John's Gospel is quite different than Matthew, Mark, and Luke. Around 90 percent of the material in John's Gospel is unique to John. The themes of John are also quite different. To fully appreciate this, examine some of the words John uses more than other Gospel writers.

FREQUENTLY USED WORDS IN THE FOUR GOSPELS

	Matthew	Mark	Luke	John
LIFE	7	4	5	36
TRUTH	1	3	3	25
WITNESS	1	0	1	35
LOVE (verb)	12	10	17	**77**
BELIEVE	15	14	9	**106**
WORLD	9	3	3	**78**
LIGHT	7	1	7	23

JOHN 11:45-57

THE PLOT TO KILL JESUS

⁴⁵ Therefore, many of the Jews who came to Mary and saw what he did believed in him. ⁴⁶ But some of them went to the Pharisees and told them what Jesus had done.

⁴⁷ So the chief priests and the Pharisees convened the Sanhedrin and were saying, "What are we going to do since this man is doing many signs? ⁴⁸ If we let him go on like this, everyone will believe in him, and the Romans will come and take away both our place and our nation."

⁴⁹ One of them, Caiaphas, who was high priest that year, said to them, "You know nothing at all! ⁵⁰ You're not considering that it is to your advantage that one man should die for the people rather than the whole nation perish." ⁵¹ He did not say this on his own, but being high priest that year he prophesied that Jesus was going to die for the nation, ⁵² and not for the nation only, but also to unite the scattered children of God. ⁵³ So from that day on they plotted to kill him.

⁵⁴ Jesus therefore no longer walked openly among the Jews but departed from there to the countryside near the wilderness, to a town called Ephraim, and he stayed there with the disciples.

⁵⁵ Now the Jewish Passover was near, and many went up to Jerusalem from the country to purify themselves before the Passover. ⁵⁶ They were looking for Jesus and asking one another as they stood in the temple, "What do you think? He won't come to the festival, will he?" ⁵⁷ The chief priests and the Pharisees had given orders that if anyone knew where he was, he should report it so that they could arrest him.

THE SPIRAL

At this point in His journey, more and more people were believing in Jesus. With the movement growing, the Sanhedrin—the supreme court in ancient Israel—along with the chief priests and the Pharisees, worried that things were spiraling out of control.

Note that they didn't question Jesus's power or claims in this. Fresh off of the seventh sign—raising of Lazarus from the dead—Jesus's divinity didn't appear to be an open question. Rather, this was a political strategy to ensure Rome didn't intervene in their affairs. Jewish leaders weren't concerned with whether or not Jesus was right; they just wanted to preserve their political standing and status.

These would be some of the men who convicted and ultimately crucified Jesus. This should serve as a warning to all of us about the very real temptation to put anything over our relationship with Jesus.

By now, Jesus's signs and the significance they carried, including the potential political upheaval that was at stake, had made Him a wanted man. Talking among themselves, the Jews wondered if Jesus would be seen (and subsequently captured) at the Passover, where all Jews would be seen.

As committed as these leaders were, they wouldn't thwart Jesus's plan. Nothing could stop Him from making His way to the cross. Even the evil around Him had a timing and a purpose.

From here on, there was a shift in Jesus's ministry that would take Him to the hill of Calvary, where He would do as He promised and sacrifice Himself for His people.

Jesus's earthly ministry had led to this moment;
He would soon turn His eyes to the cross.

REFLECTIONS

What had Caiaphas prophesied in John 11:51-52? What implications does his prophecy have for the nature and scope of the death of Jesus?

Why would someone who sees what Jesus has done and is doing continue to deny Him?

INSIGHTS

The Sanhedrin were the judicial rulers of Israel, kind of like the supreme court. They appointed the high priest, made rulings on laws, and combined political and religious functions. Caiaphas was the high priest who would eventually preside over Jesus's trials. He was a part of the Sadducees—a group of religious leaders who were often wealthy and dove deep into politics, typically trying to appease Rome. Sadducees deny any existence of an afterlife and anything from the spirit world. Pharisees were typically middle-class, non-elite leaders in the church who had a deep devotion to the Torah and the oral traditions, upholding the law in their personal lives better than any other group.

DAY
41

PAUSE & LISTEN

Spend some time reflecting over the week's reading.

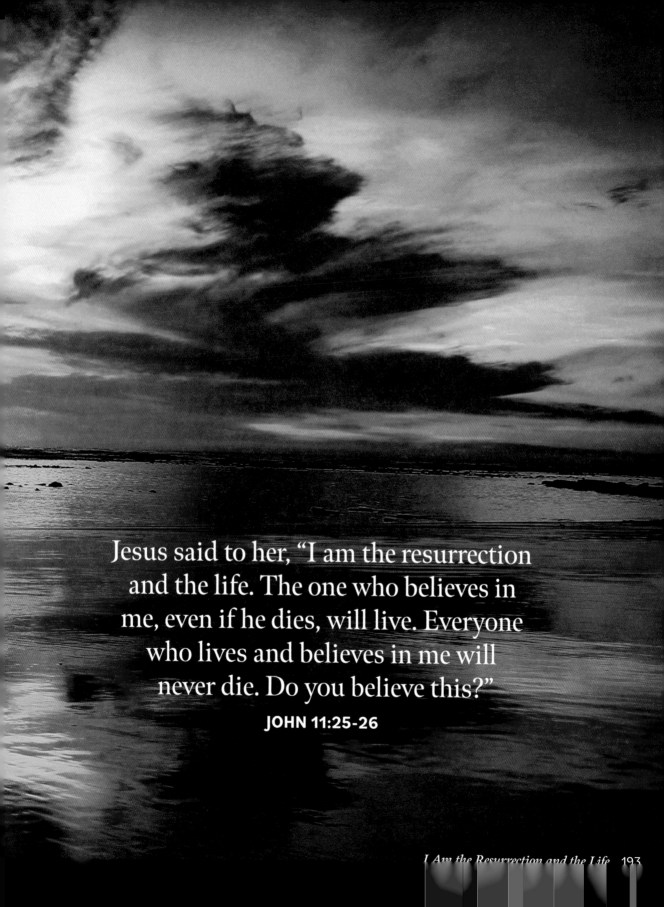

Jesus said to her, "I am the resurrection and the life. The one who believes in me, even if he dies, will live. Everyone who lives and believes in me will never die. Do you believe this?"

JOHN 11:25-26

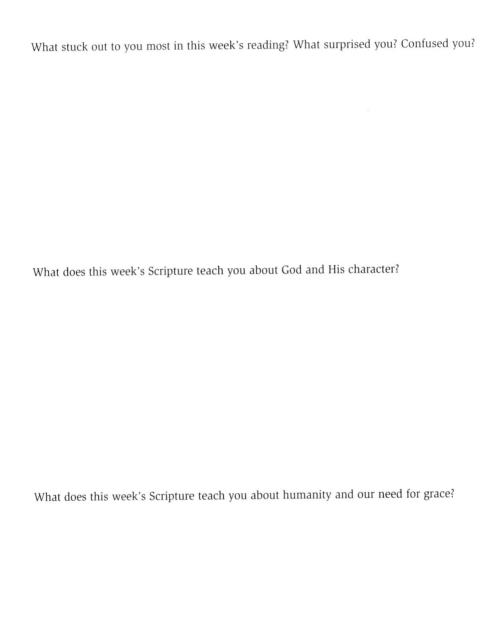

REFLECTION

Use these questions for personal reflection or group discussion on John 10:22–11:57.

What stuck out to you most in this week's reading? What surprised you? Confused you?

What does this week's Scripture teach you about God and His character?

What does this week's Scripture teach you about humanity and our need for grace?

How does this week's Scripture point you to Jesus?

How has this week's reading caused you to think about life and death? Since Jesus really is Lord of both, how should we live differently?

PRAY

Reflect on Jesus's power over death. Where do you need His resurrection power in your life? Pray for that, and appeal to the same Jesus who still has that power!

WEEK 7

I WILL DRAW ALL PEOPLE

In Jesus your questions
are answered.

This week in chapter 12 concludes the book of the signs. Throughout his Gospel, John has laid out a compelling case for Jesus as the Messiah. He has shown us seven signs—each one leading us to the point where we fall down and worship or reject Him.

The evidence gathering has ended. The conclusion has been reached.

It's here that Jesus turned toward the cross. He would enter Jerusalem for His last week of life and teaching to do His greatest work of all—dying for the sins of the world and rising from the grave three days later.

The question for us is—will we believe in the One God has sent?

JOHN 12:1-11

THE ANOINTING AT BETHANY

12 Six days before the Passover, Jesus came to Bethany where Lazarus was, the one Jesus had raised from the dead. ² So they gave a dinner for him there; Martha was serving them, and Lazarus was one of those reclining at the table with him. ³ Then Mary took a pound of perfume, pure and expensive nard, anointed Jesus's feet, and wiped his feet with her hair. So the house was filled with the fragrance of the perfume.

⁴ Then one of his disciples, Judas Iscariot (who was about to betray him), said, ⁵ "Why wasn't this perfume sold for three hundred denarii and given to the poor?" ⁶ He didn't say this because he cared about the poor but because he was a thief. He was in charge of the money-bag and would steal part of what was put in it.

⁷ Jesus answered, "Leave her alone; she has kept it for the day of my burial. ⁸ For you always have the poor with you, but you do not always have me."

THE DECISION TO KILL LAZARUS

⁹ Then a large crowd of the Jews learned he was there. They came not only because of Jesus but also to see Lazarus, the one he had raised from the dead. ¹⁰ But the chief priests had decided to kill Lazarus also, ¹¹ because he was the reason many of the Jews were deserting them and believing in Jesus.

A TALE OF TWO HEARTS

John 12 begins the last week of Jesus's life on earth. Jesus traveled to have dinner with Lazarus and his sisters, Mary and Martha. In an act of worship, Mary poured perfume on Jesus's feet. Everyone in the room might have gasped because this expensive oil that was normally poured on the head was poured on the feet. This was an act of service and humility. Mary displayed how much she loved her Savior and valued what He came to do when she anointed his feet, "The feet of the herald, who proclaims peace, who brings news of good things, who proclaims salvation" (Isaiah 52:7).

This pound of perfume would've cost about one year's wages. If we're honest, it's easy to feel like such an extravagant gift is wasteful. You might find yourself identifying with Judas Iscariot's attitude. Though his concern was insincere, it's easy to doubt or thumb our nose at lavish offerings and acts of service.

The most important thing about this offering is that Jesus accepted it with gladness. He saw the expense and extravagance and realized Mary had sacrificed her best for Him.

Jesus knew He was headed to the cross soon and received this gift as an act of worship. Pouring out her best on the feet of Jesus was not a waste for Mary, nor was her extravagant act wasted on those in the room. Extravagant worship isn't a waste today either—when we bring our best to Jesus and offer it up to Him as a sacrifice, He will do far more with our lives than we could.

In this moment, He was being prepared as a sacrifice for us.

Jesus deserves and accepts our extravagance.

REFLECTIONS

What does Jesus's response to Mary help us learn about service and extravagance?

How does Mary's act of worship compare and contrast with your posture of worship week in and week out?

INSIGHTS

Nard is a plant that was prized for its fragrance. In biblical times, the plant grew in the mountains of China and India. It can get up to three feet tall, and has a small pink flower. Once prepared, it was used as a medicine, an incense oil, and for preparing a body for burial. In the Bible, we can trace it as far back as King Solomon in Song of Solomon 4:12-14, where it's listed as a spice used to describe the husband's bride. Because of its scarcity and how far it would have to be shipped, nard was very expensive. Here in John 12, Mary's nard bottle would've cost a year's wages!

THE TRIUMPHAL ENTRY

¹² The next day, when the large crowd that had come to the festival heard that Jesus was coming to Jerusalem, ¹³ they took palm branches and went out to meet him. They kept shouting:

> "*Hosanna!*
>
> **Blessed is he who comes in the name of the Lord — the King of Israel!**"

¹⁴ Jesus found a young donkey and sat on it, just as it is written:

> ¹⁵ **Do not be afraid,**
>
> **Daughter Zion. Look, your King is coming,**
>
> **sitting on a donkey's colt.**

¹⁶ His disciples did not understand these things at first. However, when Jesus was glorified, then they remembered that these things had been written about him and that they had done these things to him.

¹⁷ Meanwhile, the crowd, which had been with him when he called Lazarus out of the tomb and raised him from the dead, continued to testify. ¹⁸ This is also why the crowd met him, because they heard he had done this sign. ¹⁹ Then the Pharisees said to one another, "You see? You've accomplished nothing. Look, the world has gone after him!"

JESUS PREDICTS HIS CRUCIFIXION

²⁰ Now some Greeks were among those who went up to worship at the festival. ²¹ So they came to Philip, who was from Bethsaida in Galilee, and requested of him, "Sir, we want to see Jesus." ²² Philip went and told Andrew; then Andrew and Philip went and told Jesus.

²³ Jesus replied to them, "The hour has come for the Son of Man to be glorified. ²⁴ Truly I tell you, unless a grain of wheat falls to the ground and dies, it remains by itself. But if it dies, it produces much fruit. ²⁵ The one who loves his life will lose it, and the one who hates his life in this world will keep it for eternal life. ²⁶ If anyone serves me, he must follow me. Where I am, there my servant also will be. If anyone serves me, the Father will honor him.

THE KING IS HERE

Crowds lined the streets to welcome to Jesus in to the Passover feast—and these were no small crowds. "Josephus estimated the Passover crowd at 2,700,000, suggesting they would have been driving over a quarter of a million lambs into Jerusalem for this Passover feast."[11] People were shouting "Hosanna!" and calling back to Psalm 118:25-26, where the psalmist cried out for God to save His people. This was a psalm known to point to a coming Savior; these crowds were beginning to recognize and honor Jesus as the Messiah.

Jesus rode into Jerusalem as the embodiment of peace and victory, the very symbols that palm branches stood for—and Jesus came to bring both. By riding in on a donkey, Jesus fulfilled the prophecy from Zechariah 9:9—and people recognized this fulfillment. Jesus knew what He was doing and what riding on a donkey symbolized. Jesus declared and the people confirmed that He was the triumphant King.

But unlike other kings, this King did not ride into town to celebrate Himself and His accomplishments; He came to give Himself to the crowds who were praising Him now but would quickly turn on Him. Those yelling "Hosanna" would soon yell "Crucify Him" with equal fervor.

Jesus rode into Jerusalem to surrender His life to the will of the Father for the benefit of those who rejected Him. Jesus shows the path to peace and victory is in surrender. When we surrender our lives in this world, we find true life in eternity.

Jesus rode into Jerusalem to surrender His life to the will of the Father for the benefit of those who rejected Him.

REFLECTIONS

Read Psalm 118 and Zechariah 9, the two passages that the crowds cited as Jesus entered Jerusalem. What parallels do you make between those passages and the scene in John 12:12-26?

Reread John 12:25-26. What part of your life do you still need to surrender to the King?

Over what situation do you need to cry out to God and shout "Hosanna"?

JOHN 12:27-36a

²⁷ "Now my soul is troubled. What should I say — Father, save me from this hour? But that is why I came to this hour. ²⁸ Father, glorify your name."

Then a voice came from heaven: "I have glorified it, and I will glorify it again."

²⁹ The crowd standing there heard it and said it was thunder. Others said, "An angel has spoken to him."

³⁰ Jesus responded, "This voice came, not for me, but for you. ³¹ Now is the judgment of this world. Now the ruler of this world will be cast out. ³² As for me, if I am lifted up from the earth I will draw all people to myself." ³³ He said this to indicate what kind of death he was about to die.

³⁴ Then the crowd replied to him, "We have heard from the law that the Messiah will remain forever. So how can you say, 'The Son of Man must be lifted up'? Who is this Son of Man?"

³⁵ Jesus answered, "The light will be with you only a little longer. Walk while you have the light so that darkness doesn't overtake you. The one who walks in darkness doesn't know where he's going. ³⁶ While you have the light, believe in the light so that you may become children of light."

LIFTED UP

We see again both Jesus's humanity and divinity on full display. Knowing He would soon die, He found His soul troubled, yet resolved not to back down. God the Father honored Jesus's request by announcing that He would glorify His name through His Son.

Then Jesus let the crowd in on what sort of death He would experience: one where He would be "lifted up." This was a reference to Jesus being lifted up on the cross and glorified by the Father, which Jesus also alluded to in His conversation with Nicodemus (see John 3:14). Jesus was lifted up on the cross so that we might see the horror and the cost of our sin as well as the grace and compassion of our Savior.

Jesus had to die because God is holy and sin is an offense to His character. In His goodness, God has set up boundaries in our lives. These boundaries define what is right and wrong and are also designed for our health and growth. Transgressing God's boundaries is sin. And the price for sin is death—physical death and spiritual death.

This is why we need a substitute. Jesus came as a Man and lived the life we could not live, died the death we deserved but was vindicated by God and raised on the third day. When people look to Jesus lifted up on the cross, admit their sinfulness and place their trust in Jesus to save them, they find the kind of freedom and eternal life we've been reading about throughout this study.

Believing in the Son of God as our Messiah and Savior means placing our whole lives into the hands of Jesus so that we, like Him, become children of light (see v. 36).

Because He glorified God, when we look to Him and pursue Him as His disciples, we glorify God too.

Jesus was lifted up so that He might
draw all people to Himself.

REFLECTIONS

Read 1 John 1:5-7.

> [5] This is the message we have heard from him and declare to you: God is light, and there is absolutely no darkness in him. [6] If we say, "We have fellowship with him," and yet we walk in darkness, we are lying and are not practicing the truth. [7] If we walk in the light as he himself is in the light, we have fellowship with one another, and the blood of Jesus his Son cleanses us from all sin.

With that as a backdrop and Jesus's words in John 12:35-36, what does it mean to walk in the light?

How did Jesus first draw you to Himself?

Who around you do you sense that Jesus may be drawing to Himself?

JOHN 12:37b-43

³⁶ Jesus said this, then went away and hid from them.

ISAIAH'S PROPHECIES FULFILLED

³⁷ Even though he had performed so many signs in their presence, they did not believe in him. ³⁸ This was to fulfill the word of Isaiah the prophet, who said:

> **Lord, who has believed our message?**
>
> **And to whom has the arm of the Lord been revealed?**

³⁹ This is why they were unable to believe, because Isaiah also said:

> ⁴⁰ **He has blinded their eyes**
>
> **and hardened their hearts,**
>
> **so that they would not see with their eyes**
>
> **or understand with their hearts,**
>
> **and turn,**
>
> **and I would heal them.**

⁴¹ Isaiah said these things because he saw his glory and spoke about him.

⁴² Nevertheless, many did believe in him even among the rulers, but because of the Pharisees they did not confess him, so that they would not be banned from the synagogue. ⁴³ For they loved human praise more than praise from God.

THE LOVE OF PRAISE

This passage today contains two of the saddest verses in all of Scripture: John 12:37 and John 12:43.

In verse 37, we read once again about the people's unbelief. They saw Jesus do many signs and wonders, yet still didn't believe. But even this unbelief serves to make John's point. The prophet Isaiah had testified centuries earlier that the Messiah's own people would not believe Him, that He would be rejected by them. Their unbelief fulfilled prophecy.

Even unbelief does not stop or undercut Jesus, but it does help us see parts of ourselves in the crowds who rejected Jesus. It's easy for us to look at them and ask how they missed it today, but we need to ask better questions: *What are we missing right now? Where is the unbelief in our lives? Where are we missing the clear work of Jesus right in front of us?*

Or like the leaders, what are we missing of His power because we're afraid of what other people with think? Including these verses, John referenced four times when people were expelled from synagogues for believing in Jesus (see 9:22; 12:42; 16:2). Maybe that's you. Maybe you want to believe but your desire for approval or fear of dismissal overcomes your belief.

The good news is that Jesus can overwhelm and overcome our doubts and unbelief with simple faith. We can trust in what we have seen and heard. We can come to Him when we're afraid and desperate for approval. He will receive us and give us what we need.

His is the only approval we need.

Jesus can overwhelm and overcome
our doubt and unbelief.

REFLECTIONS

Read John 12:43 again. What were people afraid of? What sorts of things could cause you to love "human praise more than praise from God" (John 12:43)?

In what times and seasons have you battled unbelief? Which reality resonates more with you right now, John 12:37 or John 12:43?

How have you seen Jesus work in your life? List as many works as come to mind.

?
Questions in John

Another motif or feature of John is a curiosity about Jesus. In the beginning, Jesus's identity was obscured or hidden, but several passages feature questions meant to lead the reader to answer them and reach John's intended conclusion—the realization that Jesus is God.

JOHN 1:40-42

⁴⁰ Andrew, Simon Peter's brother, was one of the two who heard John and followed him. ⁴¹ He first found his own brother Simon and told him, "We have found the Messiah" (which is translated "the Christ"), ⁴² and he brought Simon to Jesus. When Jesus saw him, he said, "You are Simon, son of John. You will be called Cephas" (which is translated "Peter").

JOHN 4:25-26

²⁵ The woman said to him, "I know that the Messiah is coming" (who is called Christ). "When he comes, he will explain everything to us." ²⁶ Jesus told her, "I, the one speaking to you, am he."

JOHN 7:25-27

²⁵ Some of the people of Jerusalem were saying, "Isn't this the man they are trying to kill? ²⁶ Yet, look, he's speaking publicly and they're saying nothing to him. Can it be true that the authorities know he is the Messiah? ²⁷ But we know where this man is from. When the Messiah comes, nobody will know where he is from."

JOHN 7:30-31

³⁰ Then they tried to seize him. Yet no one laid a hand on him because his hour had not yet come. ³¹ However, many from the crowd believed in him and said, "When the Messiah comes, he won't perform more signs than this man has done, will he?"

JOHN 7:52

⁵² "You aren't from Galilee too, are you?" they replied. "Investigate and you will see that no prophet arises from Galilee."

JOHN 10:22-24

²² Then the Festival of Dedication took place in Jerusalem, and it was winter. ²³ Jesus was walking in the temple in Solomon's Colonnade. ²⁴ The Jews surrounded him and asked, "How long are you going to keep us in suspense? If you are the Messiah, tell us plainly."

JOHN 11:25-27

²⁵ Jesus said to her, "I am the resurrection and the life. The one who believes in me, even if he dies, will live. ²⁶ Everyone who lives and believes in me will never die. Do you believe this?" ²⁷ "Yes, Lord," she told him, "I believe you are the Messiah, the Son of God, who comes into the world."

JOHN 12:32-34

³² As for me, if I am lifted up from the earth I will draw all people to myself." ³³ He said this to indicate what kind of death he was about to die. ³⁴ Then the crowd replied to him, "We have heard from the law that the Messiah will remain forever. So how can you say, 'The Son of Man must be lifted up'? Who is this Son of Man?"

JOHN 12:44-50

A SUMMARY OF JESUS'S MISSION

[44] Jesus cried out, "The one who believes in me believes not in me, but in him who sent me. [45] And the one who sees me sees him who sent me. [46] I have come as light into the world, so that everyone who believes in me would not remain in darkness. [47] If anyone hears my words and doesn't keep them, I do not judge him; for I did not come to judge the world but to save the world. [48] The one who rejects me and doesn't receive my sayings has this as his judge: The word I have spoken will judge him on the last day. [49] For I have not spoken on my own, but the Father himself who sent me has given me a command to say everything I have said. [50] I know that his command is eternal life. So the things that I speak, I speak just as the Father has told me."

THE SUMMARY

If you've ever seen a suspenseful, dramatic mystery movie, you know that point in the story where everything comes together and begins to make sense. It's where the key to the whole story is given and everything up to this moment takes on a new meaning. Now, everything makes sense.

It's after you get this key that you want to go back and watch the whole movie again with this new lens. That's what Jesus does for everyone listening in this conclusion of the first half of John's Gospel.

Jesus had been giving clues and signs to His divinity up to this point, but now He spoke directly, saying they had seen Him they had seen God. Jesus was clear that He was sent by God to save the world and that He spoke on behalf of the Father. No more shrouds of mystery and no more signs were needed. Jesus's identity and mission were abundantly clear.

All the signs pointed to this: Jesus is God. He was the One the Jews had been waiting for, the One the prophets foretold, and the One whose signs revealed His divine identity and purpose.

Jesus came to bring light to a dark world. He is the only light that can never be covered up or snuffed out. As Jesus's life and John's Gospel move forward, Jesus would prove that He can and will banish darkness once for all by dying for the sins of all who believe in His name.

That's what the second part of the story is all about.

Jesus came to banish darkness.

REFLECTIONS

What was the most meaningful insight you had studying John's Gospel?

What step of faith do you need to take in obedience to what you've learned?

Who can you share the message of John's Gospel with?

PAUSE & LISTEN

Spend some time reflecting over the week's reading.

"If I am lifted up from the earth
I will draw all people to myself."

JOHN 12:32

REFLECTION

Use these questions for personal reflection or group discussion on John 12:1-50.

What stuck out to you most in this week's reading? What surprised you? Confused you?

What does this week's Scripture teach you about God and His character?

What does this week's Scripture teach you about humanity and our need for grace?

How does this week's Scripture point you to Jesus?

Summarize the first twelve chapters of the book of John in one paragraph.
Share that with your group.

PRAY

As we conclude this study, pray that everything you've read and processed so far would transform your life today and moving forward and that your transformation would spill over to others in love.

SOURCES

1. Adapted from: Andreas J. Köstenberger, L. Scott Kellum, and Charles L. Quarles, *The Cradle, the Cross, and the Crown: An Introduction to the New Testament* (Nashville, TN: B&H Academic, 2016), 363–364.

2. Andreas J. Köstenberger, "John," in *CSB Study Bible: Notes*, ed. Edwin A. Blum and Trevin Wax (Nashville, TN: Holman Bible Publishers, 2017), 1662–1663.

3. Adapted from: Stephen J. Wellum, "Incarnation and Christology," in *CSB Study Bible: Notes*, ed. Edwin A. Blum and Trevin Wax (Nashville, TN: Holman Bible Publishers, 2017), 1668-70.

4. Benjamin Franklin, *Poor Richard's Almanac* (New York: Caldwell, 1900), 8.

5. Stephen J. Wellum, "Incarnation and Christology," in *CSB Study Bible: Notes*, ed. Edwin A. Blum and Trevin Wax (Nashville, TN: Holman Bible Publishers, 2017), 1674.

6. Chad Brand et al., eds., "Festivals," *Holman Illustrated Bible Dictionary* (Nashville, TN: Holman Bible Publishers, 2003), 567–568.

7. Chad Brand et al., eds., "Festivals," *Holman Illustrated Bible Dictionary* (Nashville, TN: Holman Bible Publishers, 2003), 569.

8. Jon Bloom, "What Jesus Meant When He Said, 'You Must Eat My Flesh,'" Desiring God, June 3, 2008, https://www.desiringgod.org/articles/what-jesus-meant-when-he-said-you-must-eat-my-flesh.

9. Parallels between John 6 and Numbers 11 taken from: Crossway Bibles, *The ESV Study Bible* (Wheaton, IL: Crossway Bibles, 2008), 2033.

10. George R. Beasley-Murray, *John*, vol. 36, Word Biblical Commentary (Dallas: Word, Incorporated, 1999), 189–190.

11. Kenneth O. Gangel, *John*, vol. 4, Holman New Testament Commentary (Nashville, TN: Broadman & Holman Publishers, 2000), 233.

PHOTOGRAPHY CREDITS

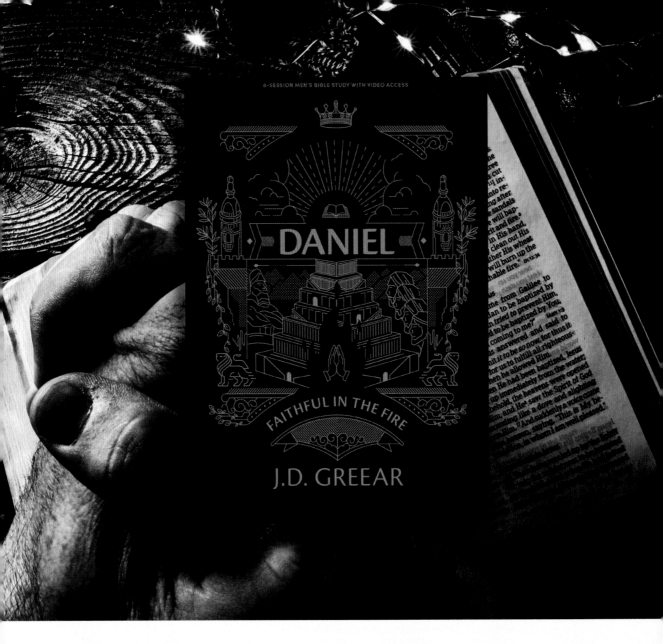

To make a difference, you have to be different.

The book of Daniel is set in the heart of a hostile, pagan empire. Yet four Hebrew men found a way to honor God, and in doing so, participated in miraculous displays of God's glory. This 8-session study of Daniel can help you and your men's group develop the courage, convictions, and habits of a faithful Christian. Perhaps God will use you to demonstrate His glory in today's Babylon.

Learn more online or call 800.458.2772.
lifeway.com/danielstudy

Step into God's beautiful story.

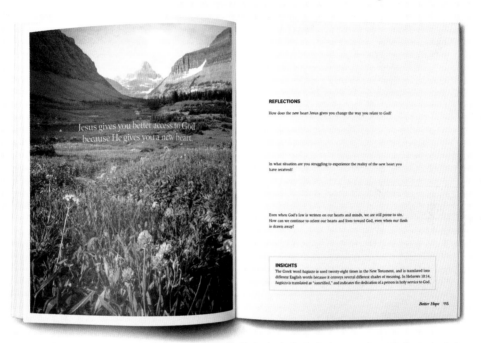

Storyteller is a Bible study series uniquely designed to be inviting, intuitive, and interactive. Each volume examines a key theme or story in a book of the Bible. Every week includes five days of short Scripture reading, a daily thought explaining each passage, a short list of questions for a group Bible study, and space for you to write down your discoveries. And new volumes are being added every year.

Learn more online or call 800.458.2772.
lifeway.com/storyteller

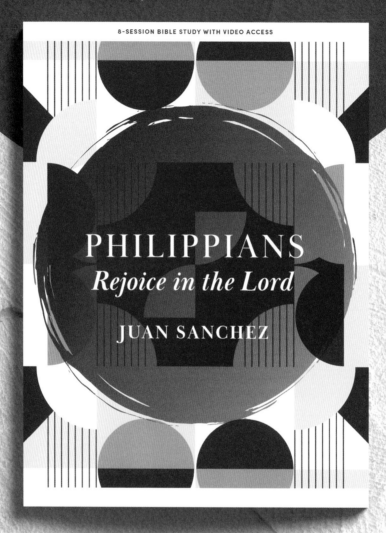

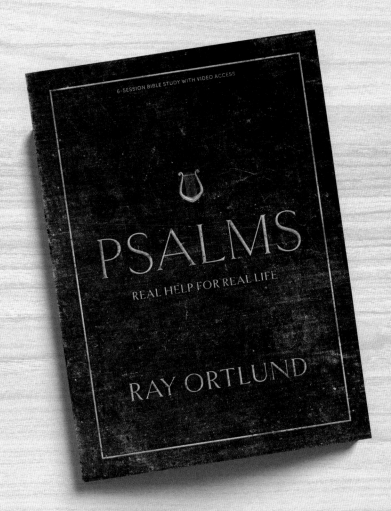

Learn to find help for all of life's circumstances.

The Psalms are filled with people venting surprisingly honest feelings toward God, whether it be anger, disappointment, awe, or happiness. This new study from Ray Ortlund will help you see that the Psalms are a place that God has provided to encounter Him and find help, rest, hope, courage, joy, and confidence for whatever you face in life.

In the beginning …

John's Gospel begins with the same three words used to start Genesis—"In the beginning." John begins his Gospel with an immediate reference to Jesus: "In the beginning was the Word, and the Word was with God." He wants us to know Jesus was part of the plan from the very start.

Just as the original creation account in Genesis took seven days, John structured the first twelve chapters of his Gospel around seven miracles.

Each sign is like holding a diamond up to the light: with each turn, rather than seeing a different diamond, you see more of its beauty in this new "creation" account.

This seven-session Bible study is designed to help you:

- Understand the purpose of miracles and see how they are signs that point us to a savior

- Dive deeper and understand key moments from Jesus's life and ministry for the first time

- See that Jesus is the true Word sent from God to give life and light to all men

- Embrace Jesus's identity as the true Son of God and only Savior of the world

ADDITIONAL RESOURCES

eBOOK
Includes the content of this printed book but offers the convenience and flexibility that come with mobile technology.

005842045 **$19.99**

Storyteller resources and additional Bible study titles can be found online at lifeway.com/storyteller

Price and availability subject to change without notice.